# MARCH FORWARD, GIRL

## FROM YOUNG WARRIOR TO LITTLE ROCK NINE

By Melba Pattillo Beals
Illustrated by Frank Morrison

HOUGHTON MIFFLIN HARCOURT
Boston   New York

hmhco.com

The text of this book is set in Centaur MT Std.

Photo credits:
Melba Pattillo Beals: ix, 2, 8, 18, 28, 77, 105, 132, 157, 158,
178, 183, 190, 199, 212, cover (foreground)
Bettmann Archive: viii, 202, 203
Jim Bowen: cover (background)
Buyenlarge: 206
Burt Glinn/Magnum Photos: 205
William Lovelace: vii, cover (center)
MPI: 201
Joyce Naltchayan/AFP: 207
Joel Rennich/UPI: 210
United States Mint: 209

Library of Congress Cataloging-in-Publication Data is on file.
ISBN: 978-1-328-88212-7

Printed in the United States of America
DOC 10 9 8 7 6 5 4 3 2 1
4500690087

To all the members of the Little Rock Nine, who marched
with me in pursuit of my dream of equality in education
for all: Minnijean Brown Trickey, Elizabeth Eckford, Ernest
Green, Gloria Ray Karlmark, Terrence Roberts, the late
Jefferson Thomas, Thelma Mothershed Wair, and especially
Carlotta Walls LaNier who stood by me through all these
years and through my journey back to the past

# CONTENTS

# PREFACE

Black folks aren't born expecting segregation, prepared from day one to follow its confining rules. Nobody presents you with a handbook when you are teething and says, "Here's how you must behave as a second-class citizen." Instead, the humiliating expectations and traditions of segregation creep over you, slowly stealing a teaspoonful of your self-esteem each day.

—*Warriors Don't Cry*, Melba Pattillo Beals
(Simon & Schuster, 1994)

During the three months that it took to write and ponder the paragraph above, I often wondered what it would take to explain this process to someone who hadn't lived it. Many of the national reviewers who wrote their opinions of *Warriors Don't Cry* mentioned this paragraph as being significant, beautifully written, and haunting. It has always stood out to me as the kernel of words that totally reflects how I feel about the life experience of an African-American.

I am writing this book in the hope of enlightening readers about the journey an African-American takes in having to grow up and live under the laws and traditions of oppression. It is an experience that indelibly imprints certain behaviors on one's brain that never, ever quite go away.

Although the experience in the South has been chronicled as being much more detrimental than that of living in the North, the bottom line is all of it hurts deeply, and all of it leaves grave impressions, which must be overcome if one is to develop self-esteem and a life purpose. In order to accomplish any goal, one must feel worthy of achieving what one seeks.

As a child, to have white people tell me both in words and by their actions that they did not feel I was good enough to

Signs like this one surrounded me during my youth. I felt smothered and choked by them.

be in their presence, ride their buses, go to their schools, go to their theaters, or drink from their water fountains made me begin to ask at age three, "Why?" At first I pondered it myself, and then I asked my parents. Their answer was this was a temporary condition that would go away.

However, my question of "Why?" got bigger and bigger as I saw the way they behaved in the presence of white people. Their facial expressions changed to humble, their words were apologetic, and their demeanor lacked confidence. They were obviously quite nervous about saying or doing the wrong thing. Everything they did or said was to gain the approval of the white people with whom they interacted. They behaved in a way that defines a word I would learn later—*kowtow.*

After a while, I decided they were afraid and that they could give no answers to my questions because they didn't really know the answers. I would learn later that segregation and oppression were not simply traditions passed down through hundreds of years, but that permission to treat us as though we were "less than" was actually defined in laws called Jim Crow.

It was signs like this that usurped my self-esteem and my hope.

It seemed to me in the beginning that none of the white people around us had any desire or reason to change. It was what had always been acceptable. Treating us as unequals was a privilege granted them by the laws of our land.

As I grew and experienced these interactions with the adults in my community and with whites outside my community, I realized that a teaspoon of my self-esteem was being extracted day by day as I struggled to survive the risky lifestyle I had to embrace in order to be safe. I came to expect this demeaning process. I didn't know how, where, why, or when it would occur, but the expectation of it boiled the fear inside me until it was overwhelming, and I realized if I didn't control it, it would eat me alive.

This book is about my experiences as a black child growing up in Little Rock, Arkansas, in the 1940s and '50s under the umbrella of the rules and traditions of my oppressors. We as black people were compelled to learn these rules in order to stay alive. They were rules that were not written down but instead handed

Here at fourteen, I was filled up to the brim with the rules that governed what my people could and could not do.

down through the spoken word from generation to generation by black folks absolutely committed to passing them on so that they and their descendants would live to one day become free and equal, to experience the freedom and justice for all in the Constitution.

# CHAPTER 1
## I'LL FIGURE IT OUT LATER

*THE FIRST THING I REMEMBER* about being a person living in Little Rock, Arkansas, during the 1940s is the gut-wrenching fear in my heart and in my tummy that I was in danger. I didn't know why exactly, but clouds of dread engulfed me every evening when day turned to night. I sensed from the very first moment of consciousness that I was living in a place where I was not welcome. By age three, I realized the culture of this small town in the Deep South was such that the color of my skin framed the entire scope of my life. It brought with it many ground rules designed to imprison and control everyone who was not white.

Of the eighty-eight thousand residents, sixty-six thousand were white, while twenty-two thousand were black. The white people and the black people lived in separate worlds that seemed to intersect only when absolutely necessary. My big questions from the beginning were "Who set up my community that way and why?" and "Why do whites get more privileges than we do—more houses, more books, more pets, and more food, more merchandise in all the downtown stores, all the police officers and firefighters, and all the transportation?" Even the city buses belonged to them.

When I felt frightened and overwhelmed, which was often, I would clench my fists so hard that my knuckles would hurt. Then I would press my open hands into my sides as hard as I could. I would let go and do it again and again until I felt in control of the terror bubbling inside me.

In order to feel safe, I always wanted to stay at home with my mother, Lois; my grandma, India; my papa, Will; and my baby brother, Conrad. Sometimes I stayed in my own room with my Raggedy Ann doll, who I called Mellie, my other stuffed animals, and my books. It was the only place I felt totally safe, as if I belonged; there was love and good in that small world

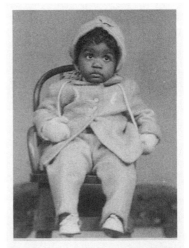

How could I know at this age that I wouldn't have the advantage of living life to the best of my ability?

for me. There was nobody there to be mean to me and call me nigger.

Our home was welcoming and cozy. There were always aromas of tasty dishes, flowers cut from our backyard in vases, doilies that Grandma India crocheted on tables, and squares of tapestry she had made on the walls. Tattered but freshly swept carpets covered the highly polished hardwood floors, and the rooms were filled with antique velvet-covered chairs inherited from my great-grandma. Grandma always hummed as she baked, especially when she prepared gingerbread men or coconut cake. I always felt loved, protected, and wanted by all the adults in my life.

On most days, my brother and I stayed in the house, pretending we were other people by dressing up or playing with paper dolls, puzzles, and blocks. When Grandma was outside, we followed her into the gated backyard, where we rolled around with our big red wagon and helped her water all the plants.

Come four o'clock in the afternoon, Grandma would let me go with her to the garden in the rear of the backyard to water what she called her four-o'clock plants. Often, I would stand beside her and wrap my hand in her freshly starched housedress as the water sprayed in my face. I never knew why she called them four-o'clocks; still I would remember for the rest of my life that this was the best time of my day. I waited for that watering all day because I could often have Grandma

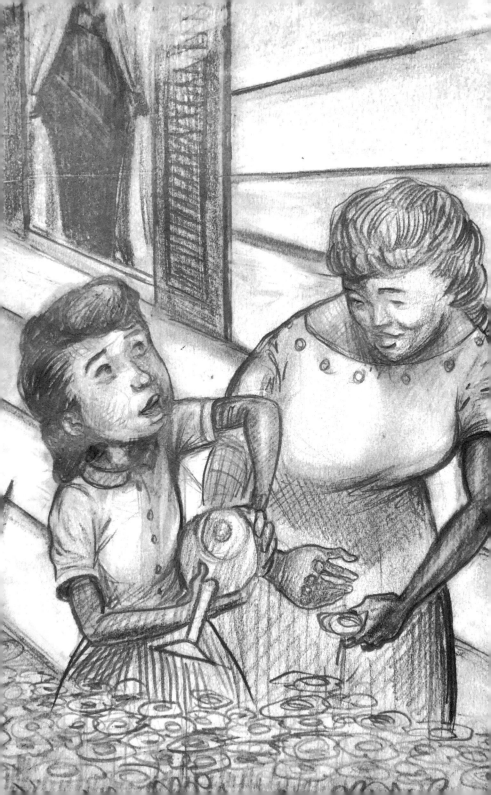

to myself. I felt the most akin to her because I resembled her more than I did my mother. She stood tall, with a medium body, and black curls about her shoulders. Her complexion was the same golden brown as mine. She made it okay for me when other people called me "big for my age" or said, "She's very dark skinned compared to her mother."

Garden time was a time when I could tell Grandma all the things—even the secret things—I was thinking about that I could not tell other people. I could ask her about what I didn't understand in the world. It was a time I could ask her where God lived. People were always talking of God, and I wanted to know where exactly He was. I wanted to go visit Him in heaven to ask Him what was going on and why we had to be treated so badly by white people. When would it end? I could ask Grandma questions like "Who is God? I don't really see Him. Is God stronger than the white people? Could He teach them to share with us?"

She would always end our talks in the garden with "That's enough for today. A wee one like you doesn't have space in her head for more deep thoughts. I don't understand why you choose to talk about all these topics. You have too much worrying in your head, baby. You're like a baby warrior! What about the joy of being a baby—about dolls and teddy bears? Let's think about other things. How about helping me with dinner, young lady?"

I would hold my breath, unclench my fists, and wait for

tomorrow. She was my very best friend and someone who always filled me with hope.

Sometimes later in the afternoon, we would listen to classical music, and Papa Will would sit on the big green velvet chair in the living room. I'd sit on his lap, and he would read to me, teach me my multiplication tables, or put together a puzzle. Often he would tell me about his sisters and brother and their life on a farm. His father was a minister, as were his uncles and many cousins. My Uncle Ben was a traveling minister.

I always felt safe when I was with Papa because to me he was as tall as the sky. He had broad shoulders and dark golden brown skin that was much like mine, as well as wavy black hair. No one was as big and protective as he was; no one ever made me feel safer than he did.

Mother Lois would come home by five every afternoon from her job at Baptist College. Some nights she would gather her books, take the chicken or peanut butter sandwich that Grandma handed her, and head out to the University of Arkansas, where she was taking classes for a bigger, higher degree—something called a master's degree. I didn't know what it really meant but figured it must be huge because she had so many heavy books. She said she would get a better teaching job and earn more money with that degree.

If Mother was studying at the kitchen table, with its chrome top and red leather chairs, I would sit at the table with her and turn the pages to look for words that I knew and pictures, which were most often not there. She would pick out a word and tell me what it meant—words like *pedagogy* and *phenomenon*. I would always giggle because I thought, *Now I know something that none of my friends know.*

"Dinner is served," Grandma would call. "Melba Joy, sit down, fold your hands, and let's say our prayers to thank God for the food we have!"

My favorite time of day was always dinner, when each of us was around the wooden table in the dining room, with warm aromas escaping from the hot dishes in the center. Grandma usually made fresh biscuits and vegetables for us even when we were only having a tiny speck of meat. Blessings, lemonade and milk, and laughter surrounded us in a joyful bubble.

On Sundays, we would have a new roast chicken for dinner. The meal would also include potatoes and a vegetable. By Thursday nights, the Sunday chicken that Grandma had roasted was down to a few threads in the soup we would eat. Yes, it was the same chicken we'd had all week, but with all the spices she added, she could make the soup smell and taste like something new and draw me to the kitchen. On Friday nights, we would have fish, and then on Saturday, we would have tuna fish casserole with green peas. We would all sit together laughing and talking and loving each other across the table. It was during these times that the world seemed perfect to me.

I just wished the white people would disappear in a puff of smoke somewhere forever.

Next was the family clean-up and a lesson of one kind or another—the alphabet, math, poems, or memorizing the sequence of the presidents of the United States in the order they served.

Although Conrad was young enough to have his self-esteem and hope, I was already sad about being trapped in oppression.

After study time, Grandma would say, "Find your pajamas and get a washbasin and take it to the bathroom. Cleanliness is next to Godliness. Start from the top down. Wash down as far as possible and then wash possible."

As Conrad got a little older, he would race me to the washbasin in the sink. If I lost, that meant I had to go get the washbowl off the back porch. Then we could bathe in our one bathroom as long as we had our backs to each other and kept the door open. We had only the one bathroom, but I was grateful that it was indoors. Some of my friends did not have that privilege, and had to go outside to use the bathroom, no matter what the weather was.

If we had finished our baths and were ready for bed well before eight, it was story time, but we had to be in bed by eight o'clock. One of the three adults would read to us. My mother told me she had read to me when I was in the womb before I was born. By age four, I was overjoyed every night to be cuddling on the bed and listening silently. When Conrad was old enough to join me, it was even better.

After story time, though, huge fears took me over. The Ku Klux Klan was a group of people responsible for much of my evening dread. Just after reading time ended, either on weekends or when we got word of trouble, Mother and Grandma would begin the ritual I watched for my entire childhood. They would close the windows, draw all the curtains and cover them with black cloth, dim the lights, and silence the radio. It brought a terror to my body that descended like a cloud and stalled anything I might otherwise do. It made me run and hide in closets, cry, and hold my breath.

"God is everywhere, and we all belong to God. He is the world," Grandma would reassure me. "He is stronger than the Ku Klux Klan. He loves us. Nothing happens to us that He doesn't want to happen."

That would always leave questions hanging in the air for me, though. "Does he want all this bad stuff to happen to brown people? Why? What have we done to deserve this treatment?"

There also came a time that when I laid my head on the pillow, I had extra worries even on top of the Klan, because I'd noticed that Mother and Papa Will were not as friendly toward each other as they had once been. They did not laugh together, hold hands, or tell jokes to each other as they had done before. The last thing I wanted was what had happened to some of my friends' families: a divorce. It worried me, and I tried to figure out what to do. When I talked to Grandma about it, she said, "Pray."

We lived on a corner of Cross Street in a four-bedroom house. Cross Street was paved, lined with small pretty white houses and many colored shutters. Sometimes working white men in their uniforms or their navy striped suits drove up and down the gravel road that ran alongside our yard, making the dust and small rocks grind under their wheels. It was a thriving thoroughfare, but if white strangers doing business came along the road during daylight, we were warned not to speak to them. It made me sad when Mexican farm workers were transported along that same road, like cattle packed in the backs of trucks, calling out to us to please marry them and rescue them.

Our street was a quiet one, with respectful neighbors who were friendly, attentive, and churchgoing on Sundays. There was Mr. Major, the plumber; Miss Austine, the hairdresser; Miss Brooks, the nurse; Mr. Elders, the dentist; and a whole array of kind working folks. Like almost all women in our community, my grandmother was a maid in a white woman's kitchen or at the Marion Hotel. My mother was a librarian at Baptist College and sometimes taught classes at other schools. Papa was a hostler's helper at the Missouri Pacific Railroad.

The people in my community always greeted my brother and me with smiles and hugs, telling us how smart and precious we were.

Sometimes during the afternoon or on Saturday, we would have friends our age—Caroline, Betty Ray, Clark, or Robert—and their mothers over to play. We didn't have lots of friends, as Mother wouldn't let us go visit others. She said home was always the safest place to be. Our friends, also around age three and four, lived a block away. Their mothers would visit with the adults, and I'd always hide and listen to them talk about our world and what white people preferred.

At times, though, I feared the visits from any other adults who would come to talk to Mother, Papa, and Grandma about what was going on outside our community. I listened in as they discussed their thoughts and tried to figure out what life-threatening activities the Ku Klux Klan might have planned for that night or the next in our neighborhood.

Grandma had explained to me that the Klan was a bunch of white men. They were law-abiding city officials by day. But by night, they put on white sheets and masks, carried fiery crosses, and did lots of evil things to our people. Sometimes they even killed a member of my community to punish him or her for being what they called "uppity." Sometimes the murders would happen for no reason at all . . . just for sporting fun.

Many of the violent, frightening things that happened to us happened after dark. I had learned early on that as long as I stayed in the places where our people were allowed to go and I didn't venture outside our community, everything seemed okay. That was, until nighttime.

Mother Lois and Grandma India spent a lot of time talking to neighbors and friends and sharing frightening stories of things the KKK were doing: taking away our people's jobs, taking away our cars, beating us, yelling at us, threatening to kill people, and yes, actually killing someone if the person did something the white people thought was disrespectful.

My little brother, Conrad, didn't understand that we were treated differently, because he was too young, but I did. It seemed to me that the grownups must have thought they could say anything out loud in front of me and I wouldn't really understand what they were talking about because I was so little. They were wrong. I took in every word, and I spent all my waking hours listening closely to the adult talk, trying to figure out their words, what they meant, and why they never spoke up, and pondering my world. How did I get here? How long did I have to stay? I imagined there must be places beyond Arkansas where my folks were treated better.

I kept secrets about how much I understood of our world. Early on, I could tell that the white people in Little Rock believed we had to do whatever they wanted us to do. I told myself that it must be that God liked them better than us. They treated us like they owned us. Whatever they said was taken as something to be heeded by my people, who repeatedly analyzed it and struggled to precisely obey their wishes. Everything they said was like a warning that if we did anything they considered wrong or said anything rebellious, bad things would happen. Everything they didn't like was punishable. Their personal opinions ruled us—there seemed to be no authority in charge to direct them as to what was fair.

The terror that this caused would haunt me all my young years.

# CHAPTER 2
## WHEN FEAR COMES HOME

**MY FEAR OF WHAT WHITE PEOPLE** might do to my family or to me was becoming a monster. Whenever neighbors or relatives came to talk about the bad things white people were doing, it was like adding height and weight to this monster that lived in my mind. Each person seemed to come to our door with a new, unique story of what horrible things could happen. I began to see these possibilities lurking in my mind's eye.

I became worried about potentially seeing white people outside and fearful they would want to come inside my house. It felt as though the adults all around me were worried most of the time too. When unknown white people visited our community during the day, the road they entered on was observed and the message of their coming was passed door-to-door by telephone, bicycle messengers, or messengers running on foot. (Some of us still did not have telephones.) It felt to me as though the Klan could come by day, and they would check each house for secrets or for behavior that might offend them. I couldn't figure out why it was such a big deal to them. As time passed, I began to understand that no one in our community could control, stop, direct, or quiet the white people who surrounded us.

Grandma often warned us not to talk with white people, especially not white people like the milkman who delivered to us. Mama was beautiful, with her fair skin and hair like silk that reached down beneath her waist. She was thin and statuesque, and white men said she looked as though she was Indian or Hawaiian. They said what I knew for certain: that she looked like she didn't belong in our neighborhood or in our household. She looked like one of them. I never discussed it with anyone, but I knew very well because friends and relatives also told me the same thing.

When the white milkman came to deliver milk, he began what Papa called "flirting": The milkman would touch her on the breasts and reach for her bottom, while he would say things to her like, "What are you doing here with these people? You must belong with us." Mother would say, "No, no, I do belong here," and would try to close the screen door between them. But she also could not fight back too much or make this man angry for fear of what he would do if she did.

Sometimes, I was frightened during the afternoon when a white insurance man visited my house. It agitated me to watch him giggle at mother and talk to her for too long, repeating inappropriate statements. I heard one man say, "If you can't be kind to me today, little lady, I'll come back tonight and take you to be all mine." From my hiding place, in the shadows of the living room, I watched as my mother struggled to protect herself over and over again.

Papa Will said the white insurance man was shamelessly bad for flirting with my mother. Papa would be home because he went to work at five a.m. and came home early, by three. If Papa was home to watch the insurance man, I could see that he was very angry, but like Mother, he couldn't say anything. Instead, he would go into the backroom hideaway, where he would polish and load his gun as though he were going to shoot the insurance man to protect Mama. That frightened me because I knew if he used the gun to shoot that white man, the Klan and the police would come.

I remembered that when my friend Jean's father drew a gun on a white man who was "flirting" with his wife, the police came and took him and two neighbors away. We never saw those men again.

. . .

All of the contacts I saw with the whites who came to our door were tense and frightening, no matter why they occurred, because we were always afraid of doing something to upset them. Often at night, the strong fear inside me turned into a rampaging river, rushing through my mind and body. Sometimes these streams of terror, and the slightest noise outside, froze me in my tracks so I couldn't do anything as I waited for the Ku Klux Klan to ride through my neighborhood, do their awful deeds, and leave.

The sound of a car or of a group of horses at night left me feeling panicked. I knew that my people would never be out there after dark that late at night, so the noises had to be members of the Klan. My hands would shake and my heart would thump in my chest as I thought of the possibilities

I remember my home on Cross Street as my only place of safety and love—even in times when the Klan rode in our neighborhood.

of what they could do to us. Grandma insisted that we turn off all noise—the radio, the phonograph—so we could hear anyone coming to our front door. I had heard the grownups talk about a house down the block that had been burned to the ground. All six members of the family were left hanging from trees, even two toddlers.

I knew no one in my neighborhood could stop those angry white men from riding through in their white sheets, holding flaming crosses. I had never even heard anyone speak of how to stop them. The Klan was all-powerful because many of them were rich businessmen, lawmen, politicians, or even city officials by day, though they were dedicated to getting rid of us by night.

Whenever I asked about why the police didn't help and why no one could stop the Klan, Mother said it had been that way forever, and the problem was that those who might stop them as city officials or the police were probably also members.

Grandma would say, "If they knew better, they would do better. Two wrongs do not make a right. You cannot hate them. We must pray for them. After all, we are all children of God—only He will come to rescue us all."

Still I could not help thinking, why not fight back? Why couldn't our men get in cars and go to the white neighborhoods to retaliate? Why couldn't we use the guns to defend ourselves when they came to our neighborhood? Why were we just waiting on God to make things better? And how long did He want us to wait? How many people would have to die before the rescue happened?

As time passed, despite the huge monster of fear that was growing out of my body and even out of my bedroom, I noticed our family had to go outside our community to satisfy our need for food and other things. As I grew older, it was easier to take me with them than to leave me home. Yet I found these trips more frightening than anything. At home I could try to put my monster in my bedroom closet and slam the door. But outside my monster could keep growing, as I never had a way to capture it. I never had any control. There was never a time to feel safe.

# CHAPTER 3
## BLACK IS AN INCONVENIENT COLOR

*THE MOST RISKY AND UNPLEASANT* adventure outside my home when I was very young was to go grocery shopping where a white man, Mr. Waylans, owned the store. When we visited there, my tummy seized up in pain and I felt as though a block of ice was in my chest, no matter what the temperature was outside. There always were so many more white people than black people shopping in that store. I knew we had to be careful. I knew, for example, that whenever Grandma, or Papa Will, or Mother went in that store, they bowed their heads and said the words they'd taught me to say to adults, *ma'am, sir, with all due respect.* Why did they have to behave like children when white people were around? It made me so sad. The grocery store made me feel like we didn't count, like we were nobody or nothing, like I wasn't Melba. Like I was just a fleck of invisible dust flying in the air.

Grandma would put her hand around my fist, which I would ball up tight. She'd say, "Watch your p's and q's, girl, keep your mouth shut, and don't let any of those big words you know out."

We stood where we thought we would be out of everybody's way in the store. We dared not move in front of any white people or look them in the eye. If we wanted to buy something, we couldn't touch it. We just pointed, and the clerk, as soon as he had time, would pick it up for us. That meant we could be waiting a long time to collect what we came for. If we were already in the line at the meat counter and a white person came into the store and wanted to get something there, we had to stand aside and let them go first, even if it meant that there wouldn't be any meat left for us. I hated how Grandma curtsied and stepped backwards when this happened.

If we were in the checkout line to pay for our purchases, usually only three or four things, white customers would step in front of us with full baskets just because they knew they could, and we would have to step back in silence because we knew we had to. I always tugged at Grandma's arm, wondering why she would just step aside. But when I asked Grandma about it, she would say, "Silence is golden, child."

As we got to the checkout, I noticed that the white people

would hand their money directly to the cashier. When it was our turn to pay, the cashier would tell Grandma to lay the money down on the counter, and he would pick it up from there, as though he would catch a disease from her money. Once I even saw a clerk take a handkerchief from his pocket and use it to pick up her money. That made me very angry.

I was always so glad to get out of the store. I felt like I was in a trap there. I wanted to be in a place where I was free. It was like someone had written over the grocery store door, over each package of food, YOU ARE NOT WELCOME HERE. I heard it in the voices of the clerk who called out, "Aintie, what are you looking for today? Remember, you are not supposed to touch anything. Let me know what you need and I'll grab it." Aintie was what white folks called our women to avoid using courtesy titles like Mrs. or Miss.

Grandma would just take my hand, and she would talk to me as we walked home about why she let the grocer speak to us that way, and why we couldn't talk back and tell him to treat us like humans. Every time I asked Grandma India why the white people owned everything, why they did not want to share, why they always threatened us, and why she behaved as though she was frightened, the answer was always the same. "In God's time; be patient."

My response to oppression was the same as always: to squeeze my hands as tight as I could and press them against my sides to push the fear back. It was almost as though, by doing that, I could push the white people far away so they wouldn't be in charge of me or anyone else anymore.

Following my fourth birthday, I began to venture beyond just the grocery store, and go on more adventures into the outside world. Just before Christmas that year, we went to the stores in downtown Little Rock, where I saw bright Christmas lights, large plants, nice furniture, and pretty pictures on the walls. All of these sights made me smile. My smile faded, though, when I noticed the many angry, disapproving faces of all the white people who didn't want me to walk or stand near them or touch anything.

There were so many items for sale in the department store that I just wanted to touch one of them. Even though I didn't have anything on my hands, no sticky stuff, Grandma snapped, "Don't touch anything." She snatched my hand and squeezed it hard. "We are not allowed to touch anything before we purchase it." I wondered why. I could see white people, even the children, touching whatever they wanted. Who said it was okay for the white folks to have permission to touch everything whenever and wherever they wanted?

I stood in front of one of the store mirrors pondering my skin color. Was there some way I could become white? Why was I this color instead of what was popular, adored, and considered okay? This topic had become the center of my thinking because all the adults around me were always talking about what it meant to be white or, among our people, light skinned. There was a wide range of color in my family, and Grandma always said, "You must be proud of your skin color. Color is no way to measure the value of a human being." Nevertheless, I noticed that despite what she said, the lighter-skinned black people were treated differently, with more kindness and attention.

Even my relatives used to tell me that it was too bad that I wasn't a boy and my brother the girl, as he was very light skinned and looked like my mother, while I was darker skinned and looked like my father. So, from the beginning they were putting a value on skin color, while Grandma was telling me it didn't matter. It felt as though everybody around me was focused on one color, white.

"If you just be quiet and behave, we'll walk down to the five-and-dime store," Grandma said when she saw me looking in the store mirror. The five-and-dime was my very favorite store because it had things we could afford to buy and we always came home with something new in our hands. The salespeople seemed friendlier there and didn't shout us down anytime we touched something. When first I saw the five-and-dime's lunch counter as a little girl, I was in awe. It had five stools and a fancy railing. Sitting on top of the counter were machines that went *whizz, whizz,* and I couldn't help looking at them and wondering what they did. One of the

clerks was holding a strawberry ice cream cone! I strained to pull my hand away from Grandma. Mother said, "Stop, Melba." Then I saw the sign. WHITE . . . I could read the first word, but I couldn't read the second word: ONLY. It wasn't in my daily reader. That's when Mother told me the whizzy machine and ice cream cones were only for white folks.

"Those people again," I shouted aloud. "Those people!"

"Shush," whispered Mother as she put her hand over my mouth.

On the way home, I thought about those pretty things I had wanted to touch. I thought about how the white people could come into our community and do whatever they wanted, whenever they wanted. We were restricted from going into their communities by large numbers of signs designating NO COLORED FOLKS AFTER DARK, or NO COLOREDS AT ANY TIME, or WHITE ONLY. By this time, it seemed to me the white folks had everything—the transportation, the housing, the grocery stores, the downtown department stores, and even all the policemen and firemen. At first it seemed as if there was nothing anybody could do about it and that black was just an inconvenient color.

I asked myself who had time to go around and write WHITE ONLY on the water fountains, these stools before me, and all the stuff on the street. Who had all those signs, and who decided where they should be put up? And what were we going to do about it? I hated those signs. How could we wrestle them away from their creators, put them in a big pile, and burn them, and then put up our own signs? FOR COLORED PEOPLE ONLY . . . PEOPLE OF COLOR WELCOME HERE . . . ALL MAY COME HERE. These were the signs I wanted to see.

I continuously felt my people had been chosen to be treated with harsh disrespect. I was unwilling to accept that as a message from God. We

Mother (pictured here with Conrad and me), no matter our age and no matter that she worked a full-time job, was always determined to give us her full-time attention. Her rules on how to behave as we began venturing out more into the world were detailed and always present.

were God's perfect children, and He loved us, as they told us every Sunday.

When we got home, I wrote the signs I wanted in my lined-paper tablet with the Indian head on the front, using the pencil Grandma sharpened for me. She painstakingly took the time to show me how to write the alphabet that would spell out those words.

And, then I thought about it: Wouldn't it be better if we could share things? Grandma kept telling me I had to share with my brother. She told me that we were all, black or white, God's children, and His resources were put on earth for us to share. We need not claim anything and be stingy with it.

"If God wanted us to share, why didn't He make the white people share?" I asked over and over.

So I also wrote in my tablet, Y'ALL COME . . . EVERYBODY WELCOME. Then it could be as our friends said it was in California, or as my Uncle Cody and Uncle Max in New York said, where everybody was welcome in churches, grocery stores, restaurants, nightclubs, and parks. White people and black people there even sat beside each other and talked to each other.

I saw no place like that in Little Rock until Mother took my brother and me to visit the Baptist College library, where she worked. There weren't any WHITE ONLY signs anywhere, and even though it was a college for our people, there were some white people working there.

Our people worked alongside those white people. At first I wondered why the white employees did not say bad things to me. I found it difficult to talk to them because I didn't know what to say and I didn't know what they would say or if they would hit me. When I asked Mother why they didn't act like that, she said it was because they were decent human beings, members of the Baptist organization, who understood we were equal.

Often the hallways were empty, and Conrad and I could run back and forth enjoying ourselves before we went into the library to sit quietly at a table and spend hours looking at books. My heart filled with joy at Baptist College because everybody I met was very sweet. It was one of the few places that made me feel safe. When we ran up and down the stairs and across the grass, no one frowned at me or ever shouted, "Nigger."

Despite this, we kept our trips outside our community to a very small number. I don't think Mother, Papa, or Grandma wanted to go outside our neighborhood any more than I did. It was so clear they were uncomfortable. I always noticed that as we began these trips, they were nervous and not certain whether we should be going at all. It never failed that Mother lectured me about what she called "public decorum": Don't be loud and brassy, check your clothes for cleanliness, and for certain don't step in front of a white person or speak to one without being spoken to first. Of course, it went without saying, don't touch anything. I sometimes wished I were my little brother, Conrad, because she never lectured him.

# CHAPTER 4
## A HEAD FULL OF QUESTIONS

*I OFTEN COMPLAINED TO PAPA* about going into public and all the WHITE ONLY signs. I asked why couldn't we touch anything. Most of the time, Papa had answers that made me smile and think everything was going to be all right.

He said, "Tell you what, little angel, let's collect all our possessions and put them in a boat and float away to an island where we're in charge. Then we would be separated from the Little Rock white people. The police couldn't threaten to take us if we did anything they ruled wrong. We'd be safe from the KKK, as the Klan couldn't ride over water with their horses or their cars."

If we did this, I wouldn't have to be worried about the bad things that would happen to us next. I asked Papa if we could buy a boat. Could we afford it? He said we wouldn't have to, as he knew how to build a boat.

When I talked to Papa about our way of living with white people, he would say, "We may have to leave this godforsaken place." I knew I'd be safe traveling with him if we did. He could build things, fish, hunt for food, cook outside, and he had a shotgun. I felt he was strong enough to build a life with us somewhere else where we all could be free. So why did we stay in Little Rock?

When I talked to Mother about it, she said, "We stay in Little Rock because we have lived here all our lives in the only home we really know. All our jobs and family are here. It would be difficult to pick up and live somewhere else unless we found a pot of gold at the end of a rainbow. Besides, Grandma and I have faith that God will change things soon."

What Mother said made me very unhappy because I felt God was taking too long to improve things.

It looked to me as though the whole black community was standing around doing nothing while the white people were taking advantage of us. I could see clearly how it controlled the way our community in Little Rock conducted itself. I was beginning to see how we judged ourselves the way they judged us. I listened in as adults spoke about what they thought of themselves and other community members based on color.

I hoped friends and relatives wouldn't ever talk about how I didn't have light, café au lait skin like Conrad did. I was tired of hearing it. The church ladies and Grandma's friends repeated the same things over and over, making me feel ashamed, and making me question my skin color. Was I not considered as pretty as he was, simply because my skin was darker? This topic had occupied my thinking for a while because all the adults around me were always discussing what it meant to be white, or the advantages of being light skinned among our people. It made my heart hurt for them to talk about me that way. It made me not want to be Melba any longer.

If I wanted to be treated better and accepted in the entire world, was there a way of changing people's minds? All the blood relatives I knew at the time fell into a range of color. My grandmother was five feet ten inches tall, and her skin was the same as mine, darker than Mother's and lighter than Papa's. The rest of the people in my community, church, and school also fell into a wide range of complexions. Grandma said they were all the colors of God's rainbow, a tapestry that made me feel that skin color should not be the measure of one's value.

Still the fact was that skin color controlled most of Little Rock life. The white people could come and go whenever and do whatever they wanted in our community. We were restricted as to where and when we could go into their community. The color of our skin attracted their attention and made us immediately identifiable. I felt that stepping outside my black cocoon was a huge risk.

What made my fear all-consuming was the fact that I observed in many instances that my parents and all the other adults who were supposed to protect me were unable to protect themselves. I called the fear I felt every day of my life "Little Rock feelings."

Since the policemen and the firemen were all white, I feared that they would do nothing to save us in any big emergency. They never, ever came to our neighborhood unless it was to pick one of us up and take us away. Late one afternoon while helping to water the lawn, I asked Grandma, "Are there firemen and police who are our color?"

"Not yet, sweetheart," she said. "God will bless us with public safety people soon."

I thought that these groups were supposed to serve and protect us, but they ignored calls from our neighborhood.

When our family car once hit a large garbage bin and caught on fire, I was so frightened as the flames whipped the same side of the car where Grandma was sitting in the back seat. It was hard for her to get out because there was no back door. It was our dark blue 1941 Chevy coupe, and you had to

push the seat forward to get out. Mama ran across the street to the church door and pounded on it. Two men came out and went right to help Grandma. They pulled her out and laid her on the ground before they sent Mama back to get more help from the church.

Three more men came out and got buckets of water. The flames grew bigger and wider as I drew back, fearing what was going to happen. They never gave up. Instead, they ran back and forth with buckets of water, all the while giving what Grandmother called their personal best. Meanwhile, one of the gentlemen helped Grandmother up and over to the church with Conrad while I stayed with Mother.

By the time the fire was out, there were about ten men helping. Everyone knew there was no need to call the city fire department, which would have had all the equipment needed to put out the fire quickly and take care of Grandma. The only reason white men came into our neighborhood was to hurt us. They never came to help us.

# CHAPTER 5
## A CHURCH FULL OF ANGELS

**WE WERE MEMBERS OF BETHEL** African Methodist Episcopal Church. We attended on Sunday and at least three other nights or days a week, though we always rushed home to get inside our house before late night. Mother and Grandmother sometimes took me to churches in adjoining towns for the weekday twilight services. There would be Bible revivals and visiting preachers and good food. Uncle Ben, Papa Will's uncle, was a traveling minister who held revivals across the state.

On most evenings, my little brother, Conrad, who was by now age three, and I, at age five, sat around churches whispering to each other, playing with our paper dolls, and coloring in books with our crayons during a sermon that often got louder and louder, until I felt the urge to hold my ears.

When the adults would come and take us and the other kids for a break, we'd go downstairs to eat some of the fancy food they had prepared. It was fun, as it made us giggle. I felt perfectly safe, until we started to make our way home after nightfall. Sometimes we were compelled to drive through white neighborhoods where we didn't belong. Signs instructed us: NO COLORED ALLOWED HERE AFTER DARK. Signs, signs— keeping us out of the movie theater, all of the restaurants and hotels, some grocery stores, all of the toy stores, most car lots, and all downtown entertainment.

As I grew older, it became clear that the church was the center of our community and the headquarters of everything good among us. I looked on as church members put their strength together to become volunteer firemen, policemen, loan officers, and protectors.

I already knew the church was really important to us, because once, when Grandma told Papa that she had stretched the groceries we had in the house as far as she could and the cupboards were still empty, Papa went straight to the church. He came back with three bushel baskets full of groceries, fresh apples and oranges, garden vegetables, and two chickens. Oh, my goodness, we celebrated. It was wonderful. Besides all that, they sent a big old pot of freshly cooked beef stew. The aroma filled the house when Papa brought it in. It was steaming hot, and we enjoyed the string beans and white potatoes in the beef stew.

I know we went to church to borrow emergency money once, and someone there showed Papa how to do his income tax. On Saturdays sometimes there was a lawyer sitting in an office with a sign on the door, and we knew the nurse or even a doctor was in another office and would be there to help us as well.

Grandma got her false teeth at church after going every Saturday for a long, long time. The dentist there worked on her teeth until finally she had a new set. Watching her clean them and put them in and out, I decided that was never going to happen to me. I was always going to go to a dentist. But she said that growing up and as a young adult, she never had a dentist to go to, so she had done her best. I didn't like seeing her without her teeth, though. She looked funny, and she wasn't as pretty.

Many, many times Papa was called out in the middle of the night by the pastor or someone higher up in the church to do a special project—help put out a fire or fix a gushing water main or hide somebody who needed to be rescued or help someone who was in harm's way to survive.

Members of the church sold homemade goods there as well. Grandma sold her sweet potato pies and her shortbread, as well as the crocheted doilies she made. Mother made suits for people. I remember her with her tape measure around her neck and newspaper on the floor, on her knees with a pair of scissors, cutting a pattern out. She could look at the person and eyeball their height or weight and therefore their size, and buy what she needed to make their suit. She could tailor both men's and women's clothes. That's how she made extra money for food and Christmas and things that we needed.

Yes, church was always, from the very beginning, the center of all of my life. Everybody knew everybody else, and everybody shared and protected everybody else. All the adults would come together and chitchat over soup about the news because we didn't have our own newspaper or any other way of getting to know what was going on in our own neighborhood.

Church was where we had lessons on how to play the piano. We played basketball and made my dollies and their dresses. We girls and women didn't have any other place to get together except the church. The truth was it was a welcoming place for the whole family.

The men, on the other hand, had their own special place to meet, greet, and exchange secrets. They gathered at the barbershop for drinks and socializing—talking and sharing jokes and laughing loudly. They also shared all the possible dangers that loomed in the air because somebody had said or done something that should not have been said or done. Or maybe he was on the run to escape white people for no reason.

Papa was one of the men who had come together to form a life-saving team that would help get them out of town. On several occasions when I went with my father to the barbershop, he would have to take me home because he'd been summoned by someone in trouble to work with that team. Sometimes if they were in a hurry, I'd be given toys to play with and dragged along. They never believed that I understood their mostly frightening conversations.

When the barbershop was closed, the men would take over a corner of the meeting/eating room at church. People in need would come there for help. So, every day the church was our help center, where we exchanged used clothing, shared food with our hungry. Loans were made for emergency expenses. If we had a big fire or needed help or protection, we called our church pastor, who gathered the community men together to provide it.

In our community, if the Klan let it be known they were looking to hang a man for an infraction, my father—along with a group of our men with special skills and armed with weapons—would work to rescue them and give them food and transportation to help them escape.

It was said that the seat of any resistance activity was the church, where black people discussed how they could fight back against mistreatment. And if someone had committed a crime against you, you called the church.

Information was provided that was vital to our survival or necessary for maintaining our home. For example, people got information on available jobs and education, and shared tips and warnings about avoiding trouble. During the week, the church would act as a school that taught women who wanted a domestic job the skills they needed. Church officials also let these women know of jobs that were available. People from other countries could come to learn how to speak English and get the knowledge they needed to manage their businesses. They would help anyone who came, be they Japanese, American Indian, or Latino, and whether they were in the United States legally or not.

Churchmen and -women cared for single mothers and widows, and provided burying silks. When someone died, women would gather to wash and dress the body, while men built coffins and dug the ground for the burial. The minister would conduct services and console the family. At the very center of our community, this holy place tied us together as a working unit and made us strong.

On holidays, there were festivals, and there were Saturday soup prayer meetings, and meals were prepared for the sick and then delivered. Church was the only real place outside my home where I felt loved, happy, hopeful, protected. Church was my faith, the symbol that God was there with us all, helping us to move forward all the time.

On a sunny Saturday afternoon when I was five, that feeling of protection was shattered. After enjoying soup together, we were seating ourselves to begin the prayer session at my great-grandmother Annie's church. It was a white wooden church with a pitched roof on a hillside in North Little Rock—a town nestled deep in the woods, almost two and a half miles across the Arkansas River. It had stained-glass windows, white walls, and roughly hewn wood benches that could give you splinters if you wiggled too much, and hurt your bottom if you sat too long. It took a moment for all the seventy-five adults and ten or more children to get settled that day.

My heart jumped when I heard the doors slam and the sound of the two big posts fall into their metal cradles, one locking the door from the inside and another from the outside. Although I was only five, I knew it shouldn't be locked now, as some people would come in late, even after the sermon started. That's when I looked back and saw six men wearing white sheets and facemasks. The two in the center were holding one of our men, who was blindfolded. It happened so suddenly that I had no time to worry beforehand.

My fear exploded, though, just as Grandma and I were being seated by the usher. I could feel the terror that loomed over the church as people turned around to see these men, who had surely not come for good deeds.

One Klansman yelled out to us, "Sit down and shut up and don't move." He had a double-barreled shotgun in his hand and was turning in a half circle and pointing it toward us all. Our men did not rush to make even one gesture of defense. Immediately, like all the ladies, they put their hands behind their backs and surrendered.

Grandma grabbed me bodily and slammed me down onto the seat beside her. "Don't look," she whispered under her breath. "Turn your head and look down at the floor. Better yet, close your eyes now, child, and keep them closed till I tell you to open them."

At that moment, some of the parishioners began to cry out, "Have mercy, Jesus!" and "Take our brother home. Please don't let him suffer. Take Harvey home." Then I heard the boots of the men walking down the aisle of the church toward the pulpit. When they got three-fourths of the way down, I heard the sound of a rope being thrown over one of the beams that went across the church ceiling from right to left. I peered through Grandma's fingers as they covered my eyes. When the Klansman reached upward to grab the other end of the rope, his mask slid down a little from his face; Grandma whispered in startled words, "Oh, no, is that

Officer Nichols? Is he one of them?" Grandma was shocked because she had worked for the Nichols family and could easily identify him. She kept her head down and pushed harder on mine.

I heard the Klansmen pulling on the rope over Mr. Harvey's head and shouting orders to each other. There are lots more of our men than there were Klansmen. What were they waiting on? If they didn't hurry and go after our attackers, something bad was going to happen to Mr. Harvey. Why didn't they use the weapons they had? Although nobody other than whites could buy guns at white-owned stores, people would come down from the North and bring arms to some of our men. I saw them exchange arms and money. Some of them might be hurt in the scuffle with the Klan, but not all of them. I was so angry with them.

"Pull harder, this is a heavy nigger, pull harder," one Klansman shouted. "Stop kicking, nigger. You'll die a harder death if you kick me." There was a long, long silence. Here was another chance for our men to get up and halt the Klansmen's mean actions. Once again, fear of the consequences kept our men from acting.

Grandma pressed her hand even harder over my eyes to make certain I was not seeing what was before us. But I could hear Mr. Harvey struggling and growling. I heard him gag, very loud, for a long moment and then he was silent. That's when I realized I had met him and talked to him when he had come to our house to fix windows and the refrigerator. He was a handyman, a very nice man with a wife and children. Sometimes he had brought his son, Eddie, who was my age, with him. I began shaking all over. My heart was thumping hard in my chest. I kept silent for what seemed like forever. I wanted to shout, *There are more of you than of them! Please, please, do something! Hurry!*

After what felt to me like an eternity, we heard the Klansmen rejoicing; they had completed their task and were saying to each other, "He won't ever look anyone in the eye and whisper under his breath again. This uppity nigger has gone wherever they go when they die!"

Then it was just silent. One of the Klansmen ordered, "Tie him off. Don't let his body slip down. Leave him till we are sure he's gone off to his maker, whoever that is."

After a long time, the footsteps of the six men went toward the back door, and I heard the inside wooden beam lifted out of its cradles. They never stopped laughing and talking like they were having a party as they knocked on the door and the second set of bars on the door was lifted from outside. There were more of them out there. I felt my knees shaking. The door opened and then several other of the Klansmen's voices rose in celebration. As soon as the door slammed shut, Grandma relaxed her firm grip on my face. I opened my eyes, and I could see the people begin to rise out of their seats and move toward Mr. Harvey, whose dangling feet hung before me. I dared not stretch up to see anything higher on his body. Somehow, I knew his face would be full of pain. I felt so, so sad for him. Tears bubbled in my eyes.

The minister ordered the choir to sing, *Come to Jesus, come to Jesus right now.* Moments later, Grandma grabbed my arm again and dragged me down the aisle faster than ever before toward the front of the church where the pulpit and choir stood. The choir was singing. Ignoring all of this activity, Grandma dragged me out the side door into the dark woods. She said the Klansmen might still be in the front; we could not go to the car. We stumbled forward really fast for a long time. Finally, we made it through the pitch-black forest to Aunt Sandra's house, where we spent the night in near silence.

That night and many nights afterward for a long time, I could see Mr. Harvey's feet hanging down and the rope stretched over the rafter, and I imagined his face in my mind. I didn't talk to anyone about this because Grandma told me that if I said anything to anyone about seeing Officer Nichols there with the Klan, they would come get us and hang us, too. I thought I would never forget that scene as it replayed in my head.

I was robbed that day of one of the few places where I felt safe. I knew the truth after that. There were no real safe places. Now I knew for certain that even the church could not stop the Klan from hurting us. And, if no one could stop the Klan from hanging Mr. Harvey, then even the church could do nothing to stop the Klan from hanging me. Sometimes I felt very alone on earth, as if there were no adults to protect me.

God's house had been everything to me: a house of joy and the center of our private sanctuary—where we met to organize and pledge to support each other. But it was just another place where we could be hanged.

# CHAPTER 6
## RULES OF MY SURVIVAL

*AFTER THAT AWFUL EVENING,* the image of Mr. Harvey erased any hope of my church being safe. No longer did Saturday soup prayers make me feel joyous and peaceful because now I knew the truth. There was no sacred space. There was no space for us to call our own.

Seeing the awful end to Mr. Harvey's life frightened me from the top of my head to the tips of my toes. As a result, I knew I had to learn all the rules for survival and obey them to the letter. The white people in Little Rock were not afraid to kill us. They did not at all fear taking our lives because they didn't think of us as human beings. Instead they treated us like throwaways. My promise to myself was to survive so that

I could escape Little Rock and empower myself with enough education to come back home and change everything.

I studied the rules of interacting in the white world as a person of color. The ones I found most difficult were *don't speak to a white person unless spoken to* and *if that white person says awful things to you or about you or hits you,* DON'T TALK BACK—FOR GOD'S SAKE, DON'T FIGHT BACK.

No one ever wrote down all the rules for me. Instead, they were passed down from generation to generation by the older relatives who whispered or spoke them to me time and again. Grandma repeated the rules to me every day, and I knew for certain that I had to memorize them and not leave anything out. She even gave me frequent exams to ensure I was memorizing them. Still, there were ones I had not yet learned, and Grandma said there were often new ones. Sometimes it was easy to forget them because I was so angry and really didn't want to obey them. I wanted the adults to fight back. I wanted God to come right now and show me He loved me by fixing the problem by standing up for me.

Every time we went to town or anyplace where there were white people, it initiated her urgent voice with instructions to me. She sounded as though she was trying to cram everything in as quickly as possible so I could avoid having something awful happen to me. It seemed as if every adult felt compelled to give us young people basic instructions. Do not speak to white people unless spoken to first. Do not look directly into the eyes of a white person. Do not approach or walk near a white person unless invited to do so, and if a white person walks directly toward you, always stand far back or move aside and let them pass.

Often, I was snatched from the path of an oncoming white person, even destroying my polished saddle shoes as I stepped off the sidewalk into the mud, wondering why the white people deserved the sidewalk more than I did. Grandma would always make me take time to polish my saddle shoes. Did she know I might have to walk into the mud and spoil them?

I didn't find out about the bus rules until Grandma needed to get a medical prescription filled downtown one day and our car stalled out. I was skipping along to the bus stop ahead of her, and when the bus stopped, I got on before her. The steps were so deep that I could barely climb up. While Grandma stopped to drop our money in the change box, I took a seat right there in front across from the red-faced driver. Suddenly he lunged up from his seat behind the railing that separated him from the aisle, and threw his hand back as if he was going to slap me across my face. I ducked to the floor and began to cry.

What had I done?

"Please, sir, she just doesn't know any better because we don't really ride buses. I know our place," Grandma pleaded as she dragged me from that seat to the back of the bus. The seats were tattered, and there was an awful smell of chemicals and oil and the loud sound of the engine roaring as the bus pulled away from the curb. There were only my people packed into these seats. So, Grandma and I had to stand up at first. She held on to the overhead rails while I held on to her skirt. After two stops we got to sit across the aisle from each other. Taking a deep breath, I vowed I would never, ever ride a bus again.

I learned the white people's rules, but I could not stop myself from testing them. I wondered if they applied to us only because none of us seemed to push back. My testing of the rules had gotten me into trouble several times, but I couldn't keep myself from crossing the lines that Grandma had drawn. I was obsessed with escaping our grungy, filthy, smelly bathrooms with COLORED WOMEN marked on the doors. So, I'd tried checking out the white ladies' bathroom in a downtown department store several months before. It had not worked out at all. Several police officers took us upstairs after I had been thrown out of the bathroom and questioned us for hours.

"We know our place," Grandma told him. "She doesn't

yet know better. Please, sirs." She bowed down to them with her hands in a prayer-like position. It hurt my feelings and made me feel as minuscule as an ant to see her behave that way. The policemen's attitude toward us and the way they spoke to us made my stomach hurt. For a while it seemed they were going to arrest us and take us away forever. But why did Grandma have to behave as though she was praying to God when pleading with them?

Despite the anguish of that risk-taking move, I continued to believe I deserved to be treated equally. I believed there had to be a way out. There must be a way to make these smothering rules go away. I kept asking myself and others around me, "Why doesn't God love me as much as the white people? How come they have everything? How did they get here first? Who put the white people in charge?"

Now it was early in December when I had just turned six. All the Christmas toys and decorations were out. So, after getting the medication, Grandma and I went over to the department store where we were met by Mother and Brother. Brother and I wanted to look at toys. While Grandma and Mother were looking for a new lamp for the living room, I managed to wander a little bit away where I could see them, but they couldn't see me. Conrad and I were so tired of looking at grown-up furniture and being told not to touch it or sit on it. I wanted to look at the dollies because I wanted to choose one for Christmas. Conrad wanted a dump truck.

I wondered why all the dollies were white with blue eyes and none of them looked like me. I saw one on the shelf just above my head with fat white legs sticking from beneath her starched pink dress. There was nothing I wanted more than to touch that doll. I had to stand on tiptoes to do it. That's when a wrinkled blond clerk said, "Listen here, little nigger, take your hands off that." Then she slapped my hand. I felt a sad lump in my throat as the sting on my hand grew more intense. I looked up into her eyes.

"I just wanted to touch the leg. I wasn't going to take it away," I shouted at her.

She said, "You know you niggers aren't allowed to touch anything in the store. No one will want it after you've touched it."

I said, "You're mean, a real meanie. And your face is wrinkled and white like a clown."

By this time, Grandma must have heard my voice because she was suddenly right there, apologizing for me. I wanted to scream at her, *No, Grandma! I'm not sorry. Don't apologize!*

But Grandma went on telling the clerk that she'd work with me. "Please don't call the manager. She's just young. We know how we're to behave. We know our place. She'll learn and never do it again, I promise you."

Mother Lois had come over, and the expression on her

face made me more frightened. She was red-faced and teary-eyed. She picked up Conrad, looking scared as she did. My grandma grabbed my hand tightly, angry at me. We stood there for a moment waiting for the clerk to say something.

She did. "Aintie, consider this a Christmas gift. And leave that pickaninny home next time. Don't let me see you in this store again, or I'll tell my manager."

Grandma turned and snatched me away as we walked really fast up the aisle, past the lamps, and out the front door.

At the different stores we visited, we couldn't even try on clothing to see if things were the right size. If I wanted to buy something for myself, I was told, "Estimate a size, call the clerk, she'll pick it up, then you pay for it and be done."

"What if it doesn't fit?" I asked.

Grandma said. "There are no returns for us. As I told you, never look at anything in the stores that you are not going to pay for." Her voice was exasperated. She was very angry at me. I wondered why she wasn't angrier at whoever made those rules.

When I complained to her about the ugly behavior of that bus driver and store clerk, Grandma said, "We are all children of God. If they knew better, they'd do better. We are going to have to forgive them and be patient for our own sake until the Lord can get through to them and things change."

Whenever Grandma said, "God loves us each one as his children, and He put us on earth to share," I was feeling sad and confused because what were we supposed to share and when? Did they get God's share message? The white folks had all the stuff. They had no desire to share. I couldn't sit on the front of the bus; we couldn't swim in their pool, attend their schools, or go to their movie theaters. What was there left to share?

The more places I went in the big world, the more I disliked the signs I saw: WHITES ONLY and NO COLOREDS ALLOWED. Those signs were standing between me and everything I wanted. White folks not only refused to share with me, I was told to keep quiet because they would punish me if I complained and spoke my desire for those precious goods or privileges.

On a trip to the fabric store, I remember being thirsty and moving toward the water fountain right in front of the store. My grandmother pulled me away from it, scratching my hand in the process, as she directed me to the fountain marked COLORED. The difference between the two was that the one for whites was bright and shiny and clean. The colored one was far away and was rusty and looked as though it had long ago been abandoned on some junk pile. Surely, I would get a disease if I drank from it.

As time passed, I came to understand something I had

heard some of the elder folks I knew say: "The white man has got the colored folks in a bottle. He can put the top on anytime he wants. He can tighten the top, shake the bottle around, or open the top to let him breathe, or he can decide to throw that bottle away. It's all up to him, his choice." The lesson I learned after a while, through awful experiences and Grandma's lectures, was that nobody was ever coming to rescue me. Nobody was going to take the white people's possessions and divide them in half so we could get our share, or convince them that sharing the transportation, the swimming pool, and every other fun adventure was the right thing to do.

Again and again, my Grandmother India would tell me to be patient. "In God's time, child, He loves us all equally. Our time will come." I would think to myself, *I will not make it. What if they burn down our house? What if they do bad things to me? What if they hang me with a rope before God's time comes?*

That meant that I was now even more frightened every day of my life that I would never get access to things I longed to do, be, and have—or frightened that if I did get access, I would be punished by death. Proof positive of our vulnerability would come when I observed white people saying insulting things to Papa, Mama, and Grandma. They would even threaten us, and the adults in my life would only reply, "Yes, sir," or "Yes, ma'am."

I felt totally helpless, without any hope my life could be better. I thought to myself, *No one on this planet loves me enough to take care of me.* I felt I wasn't where I was supposed to be. By age five, I told Mother Lois, "The stork dropped me off in the wrong place. Mama, call the stork and have him come back for me and pick me up."

There had to be someplace where it was okay to be me, and where nobody else was the boss of all my people. There had to be someplace where there were none of those WHITE ONLY signs, someplace safe on earth for us. Even if we weren't in charge, we had to be equal. I would be the one to find this place, and I'd come back and rescue everyone.

I spent many hours sitting in my red wagon in front of my house, waiting for the stork to fly overhead so I could flag him down and get a ride out of Little Rock, Arkansas. During my wait time, some days the sun beat down on my head and I got a headache. *Is it not picking me up because I'm black? Or maybe I've gotten too heavy?* I thought to myself. If the stork wasn't coming, I'd have to find another way out of Little Rock. If I didn't do something, I was going to be stuck. Nobody else was doing anything, and I wanted more, much, much more.

Every Sunday after church we would go for a ride in the school neighborhoods I coveted and daydreamed about. We could drive by only in the daytime, however, and we dared not get out of our car. Just like white people held the keys to things like the merry-go-round, the swimming pool, and the movie theater, they held the keys to all the best-equipped, most beautiful schools.

One of the neighborhoods we drove through was the eight square blocks around Central High School. It was a wonderful building, at least seven stories high, landscaped with topiary bushes shaped like animals and a waterfall. It was an extraordinary compound including a gym, large stadium, outdoor fields for soccer and volleyball, tennis courts, a giant auditorium, and a library. Rumor had it that they had furnished the school exquisitely and the students and teachers had access to electronic typewriters. They also had apartments with full kitchens to teach home economics. It was considered "the most expensive, most beautiful, and largest high school in the nation" and an excellent educational facility and academically graduated a high percentage of students who went on to top universities.

I asked Mama and Grandma if I could go to that school someday. Central was so wonderful and very close to my house. They said it was not for us and that I would understand later. Papa would say, "You don't need to be asking those questions. Keep focused on following the rules so we can stay alive." The one thing I wanted more than anything else was to walk through the halls of Central High and to be invited to get my education there. I thought a diploma from there would be the key to getting out of Little Rock forever.

Once again Grandma repeated, "Wait on the Lord. You're impatient. Wait for Him. He will not disappoint."

But my question was, "How long?"

"Until the wait is over," Grandma said sitting back in the green velvet chair in the living room. She had the prettiest smile on her face, as though she was talking about something so precious that I couldn't understand how big and how important it was, but I knew that it was something wonderful.

"No human being has the power or the knowledge to rescue us. Yes, I've waited a lifetime, and I can tell you there is no miracle change. It's when He says it's time for us to be equal that we will get to be equal. We can count on God because He is all you got, all I got, and all there is. There is nothing else."

# CHAPTER 7
## DIMMING THE LIGHT OF MY DREAM

*I DID MY BEST TO FOLLOW* Grandma's instructions and tell all my secrets only to my diary, but I looked forward to days I didn't have to worry about the outside world or write about my fears. On one of those days, Conrad and I were having a day of fun with Grandma. I couldn't say anything wrong because there was nobody around to hear me.

On this very special Saturday morning, Grandma, Conrad, and I were up early puttering around. My brother and I were giggling and chasing each other around the house as silly five- and three-year-olds do. Grandma promised if we cleaned our rooms and picked up our toys, she would help us make gingerbread cookies to eat before we began playing games. That was our favorite thing to do. She used raisins as eyes and jelly beans for the nose and mouth. Once the cookies were done, she would talk in what we called her gingerbread voice and pretend to be the characters on the cookie sheet. There was a gingerbread family with a mother, a daddy, and three babies. It would always take until the cookies cooled down for her to finish her gingerbread adventure. She told us a wonderful story that day, made even more real by her gestures and changing voices to match the different characters.

I hurried through my cleanup and urged Conrad to join me so we could quickly get to the joy of our cookies and play. Then the phone rang and Grandma's smile turned into a frown. It was Miss Lisa on the phone. Grandmother worked for her as a maid during the week. She had called to summon Grandmother to work for her today. I heard Grandmother try to plead her way out of it.

"My grandchildren and I are here alone," she said first.

Then, "I have very important plans."

Finally, she said, "I don't feel one hundred percent."

Each protest brought more beads of perspiration to Grandmother's forehead. Ultimately she gave in, saying, "You do understand I'll have to bring the babies with me. Their mother is off at university having a class. I have no way of getting ahold of her."

Grandmother put the phone in its cradle as a terrible

frown settled on her face. She told us to hurry, gather our things, and come with her. She put our crayons, a notepad, and pencils in a bag, and we walked out the door, down the stairs, and across the backyard.

It had been exciting at times when Conrad and I had gone to Miss Lisa's house with Grandma and ended up playing with her children while Grandma cleaned and cooked a meal. I had learned that it was an accepted tradition in the South to have white and black children privately play together until about age six, but never in front of their white friends. We could never, ever speak to them in public.

Grandma had explained to us that by age six or eight, we would be separated by very strict lines forbidding us to ever speak to each other again, except if absolutely necessary. As we played with Miss Lisa's children up till then, there had been few reminders that we were not considered their equals. Every now and then, Miss Lisa would come in as we were playing and ask my brother and me to call her little daughter Miss Mary Lee and her son Mr. Henry, though.

This time, however, as we arrived anxious to get started with our play, Miss Lisa instructed Grandma to take us to the kitchen pantry. "They'll be all right in here for now, India," she said, glaring at Grandmother with an *I dare you to say no* look.

I wondered why we had to go in there. Was Grandma going to clean the pantry? When Miss Lisa slammed the door behind us and locked it, separating us from Grandma, I had an awful feeling inside. That's when I heard Grandma ask, "Do we have to do it this way? My babies can't be in there."

Miss Lisa responded, "I can't have those niggers playing around my children and the children of my friends. Those mothers will think I've lost my mind."

My heart skipped a beat as I sank down to sit on the floor. As time passed, I began to perspire in that small hot room. I wanted out. I could hear the children arrive for what must have been a party and hear their laughter and chatter. As we entered, I had seen the balloons and brightly colored paper hats. I wondered why Grandma had locked us in. I started to turn the doorknob back and forth over and over again to see if it was true. I knew how to behave at a party, and especially one for birthdays.

"Grandma, Grandma, let me out," I called.

She cracked the door slightly. "Shush. Honey, I won't be a lot longer—settle down—play with Brother." Then she slammed the door behind her.

"Play? Play with what?" There was nothing in that dingy room to play with, and Brother's face was beginning to cloud with sadness. Tears filled his little eyes. Besides, it was really hot in there.

"I have to poo-poo," he cried.

"I'm hungry. It's hot," I said. Then I stopped myself because I didn't want to upset my brother any more than he already was.

At age three, he didn't quite understand the situation. He was a moment from screaming when I clamped my hand over his mouth. I had to figure out what was going on. Grandma had never locked us inside of any room ever. This was when I decided to answer lots of questions in my mind and not to think bad things about her. I knew she was stressed because Miss Lisa was in charge, and Grandma needed to work for her to make money to help pay our grocery bill.

It seemed forever, though, before Grandma slipped into the door and handed us glasses of water and cookies.

"Can't we have birthday cake and balloons?" I asked.

"No, no, honey. Maybe later. I'll make you a cake. Please, please be quiet. Play tic-tac-toe." She took the pencils and paper and crayons out of her bag and threw them onto the floor, something she would never, ever do.

"Grandma, what are we doing? Let's go home," I said.

"Home. I wanna go home," Conrad mumbled in a sad, teary, helpless voice. "I want to poo-poo."

"We can't now—not now. Sorry, baby. Grandma's doing her best." I could see tears in her eyes. "It's going to be okay," she whispered.

Then she slammed the door. But I heard the music, and I had seen balloons and the cake she baked through the open door into the kitchen. We had been there a long, long time—time enough for her to bake a cake and blow up more balloons.

"Grandma, poo-poo!" Conrad screamed. I covered his mouth again with my hand.

"It's all right," I whispered. "Poo-poo in your pants. Grandma won't be angry. She loves you." I hugged him as he whimpered in my arms, and I could smell the poo in his pants. It made me cry even more.

We were both sweaty and sad. He stopped crying out loud and began whimpering to himself. I could feel tears on my cheek as we silently huddled together on the floor. I wet my pants, and it leaked through my shorts onto the floor.

I don't know how long it was, but it felt like forever before Grandma opened the door and a rush of fresh air entered the room. Conrad was red-cheeked, perspiring, and almost asleep. I was dripping wet and woozy. The party was winding down, and Grandma looked very tired and very sad. Then Miss Lisa stepped up.

"India! India, you can start the cleanup now. You don't have time for all this," she said.

"I must go now; this pantry is making my babies sick," Grandma said to Miss Lisa.

"Are you kidding me? You'll never work again if you leave me in this mess with all my friends here."

"Do to me what you need to do, but I'm leaving."

"You have to clean up!" Miss Lisa said. "If you don't, you will never get work in this community again. I'll see to it."

"I know I can get work," Grandma said calmly as she picked up Conrad and grabbed my hand, and we walked out the back door to avoid any lingering guests. We said nothing as we walked home. I didn't want to shame Grandma or hurt her feelings about how she let that white woman boss her around and had locked us in the pantry. She would never have done that on her own. Then Grandma said in a sad voice, "I love you, children, and I am doing my best."

I thought to myself, *Grandma's grown up, and she's still here in Little Rock—here without change in all these years. God has not come to rescue her. Mother Lois and Papa Will are grown up, and they're here. Does that mean God will not be coming for me? Will I grow up and spend my whole life here?* I had to find another way out of Little Rock. I had to figure a way out on my own. I knew Grandma said God was all we had, but maybe He expected something from me.

From that day forward, I never forgot about how Grandma had to lock us in that pantry to save her job and how awful that had made us feel. I knew for certain that she could not protect herself from white people, and therefore she could not protect me from them, either. She did stand up at the end, but by that time, we had been in there for four or five hours.

As we walked home in silence, I could, for the first time,

see the sadness on her face and how disappointed she was in herself. Tears brimmed in her eyes. I knew she wouldn't ever have treated us that way unless she was forced out of fear of losing her job. She must have realized now that I was aware of her awful truth—she was an adult being treated like a child by the white folks.

"Remember, both of you, I love you, and for certain God loves you," she said in a quivering voice as though she was crying inside. "I would not do anything on purpose to hurt either of you."

"Yes, ma'am," I whispered, as I tightened my hold on her hand to reassure her. What I really wanted to say was, *Why didn't you open that pantry door, take our hands, and walk out of there earlier? Why did you let her make you keep us in that hot, hot room with no potty, no water? Please, Grandma, tell me why.*

Somehow, even though I was a young girl, I knew better than to ask those questions in front of Conrad or even when we were alone. She already must have been hurting to let us see for certain that she could not talk back to that white woman and felt compelled to stuff us in a pantry. The short walk home seemed to take forever. We walked slowly, and Conrad whimpered and rubbed his eyes.

"Night-night," he said, tears streaming down his cheeks.

"First a bath and clean the poo-poo, honey," Grandma explained, pausing to hug him to her.

As we arrived home, there was more silence because there

was nothing more to say. I felt tongue-tied, queasy, and hopeless.

I went directly to the bathroom to clean up and, afterward, to my room. I fell face-down onto my bed so I could hide my loud, screeching cry deep in my pillow. I wouldn't be leaving Little Rock for a long, long time. Grandma India must be fifty years old; she had waited forever. I was five. That was so many years. I could not wait that long. I felt trapped.

I dug my face into my pillow, and for the first time ever in my life, I disobeyed Grandma by ignoring her call. I heard her asking me to help with dinner. But I dug my face deeper into my pillow, pretending I could not hear her, and cried until I thought I would dissolve into my own little puddle of tears. I did trust God, but I could not wait forever for Him to show me He loved me equally. Grandma had waited on Him since she was young, all those years, but He hadn't heard her prayers and rescued her from Little Rock.

I must have cried myself to sleep, for the next thing I felt was Grandma tugging at my ponytail and saying, "Please, honey. Get up and clean up for dinner."

As I washed my face, I could see in the mirror that my eyes were still red from crying. I took off that blouse to change it for another. I didn't want to be reminded of the day we spent in that pantry. I said nothing to Mother Lois over dinner, even when Grandma began to talk about the party Miss Lisa gave for her kids.

After that night, I felt as though a light inside me had gone out, leaving me in deep darkness. It was the light of hope that dimmed. I had lost hope that God would rescue me and that I would get to leave Little Rock. I didn't know what to do next. Should I plan to run away from Little Rock? How would I do it?

I had to somehow figure out a way to survive. I had to figure a way to keep my mind on doing what was right and to pretend everything was okay. I had to become like most of the children I knew. They didn't worry at all about such things. They neither felt trapped nor less than. They were, instead, figuring out how to be good and obedient—what I saw as failing to even explore any chance that they might deserve being equal to the white people.

I hated the feeling inside of losing hope. It was like losing my balance on earth and floating in the air like a balloon. What should I do about the future? Did I even have a future? If I had to stay in Little Rock for my whole life, I wondered if maybe I didn't want to live.

All the adults had said it would be best for me to watch my manners and be a good girl—in following God's will and obeying His rules. I vowed to myself that I would hide my hope and hide my dreams.

In order to survive, I needed to try to ignore my big wide desires to get out of Little Rock—to be equal, to have my own freedom, to see all of my people have some freedom.

That's what you had to do to be a "good" girl, Grandma had said.

From that day forward, the hopeful part of my heart was buried in sadness. I stopped complaining to my friends about being treated unfairly. I vowed to Grandma to shut up and to give my personal best in everything I did. I would no longer talk to her about how I felt about the way white people treated us.

Every day I marked another day off the calendar—one more day I had made it through life in Little Rock without complaining, dreaming of freedom, or talking about it.

While taking my daily walk with Grandma, I tried to stop myself from wanting to do things like ride a merry-go-round, swim, or go to the movies, wrestling matches, or anywhere we had to sit only in the balconies. I even put aside all the things I would say to white people when they were mean to me or my parents. I smiled as I thought of a time far in the future when I might be able to let go of my notion of collecting all the WHITE ONLY signs, putting them in a large pile, and setting them on fire.

# CHAPTER 8
## INTO THE REAL WORLD OUTSIDE

*FOLLOWING THE AWFUL SATURDAY* in Miss Lisa's pantry, I was committed to learning more about the white world and how it worked. I decided to read the newspaper that was delivered each day to our house. The lives of the white people all around us were written about in that paper.

I knew that, because Papa would come home and say, "Guess I'll sit down and read about what the white people are doing. They know what we're doing because they spy on us, but they never write about what we're doing." I was determined to know what they were doing, too, and to learn from it.

In late spring of 1946, I had a severe case of whooping cough (one that doctors thought serious enough to write up in a national journal). The whooping cough was the first thing that compelled me to venture into a bigger world where there were more white people. I'd had coughing spells and asthma for years, and had been taken to the black doctor at church before. But the persistent coughing all night and wheezing all day finally led Mother to take me to a white doctor's office, where there were many white patients but only a very few of us. She thought we might have the advantage of more healing information from the white doctor, who had been educated in a different school system.

Until that time, I had only seen white people up close at Miss Lisa's house, at the Baptist College library, in the street, or frowning at me across a store counter if it looked like I was going to touch something. In the doctor's office, I was seated not far from white people for a long time.

There was a white doctor in our town who'd recently agreed to see my people. Everybody in our community talked about Dr. James. He had agreed he would treat some black people two days per week. The waiting area at his office was divided into two sections. One had tattered chairs, scattered sets of wrinkled magazines, and wobbly tables. There were signs letting us know that colored patients could only sit here.

Through double doors and across the banister, where I often peeked, there was a much nicer room. It was well decorated with sweet pictures on the wall, leather seats with gold upholstery tacks, and brightly colored pillows scattered

among the couches and chairs. The magazines were neatly stacked on shiny bookcases with metal lamps and colorful shades. Mother and I sat for hours watching Dr. James call many white people into his office, even though we had been first to arrive. After a long wait, he called us in. Sometimes we would wait at Dr. James's office for five hours or until seven p.m., after dark, while the white people often went inside for their treatment when they arrived.

Once we were inside his office, Dr. James was nice enough. He looked me in the eye and spoke to me with a kind tone. He examined my chest and throat with a gentle touch. The doctor was the first white person who touched me and treated me kindly, as though I was human and my health really mattered to him. Still, I never got over the shabby waiting room and the long wait I had to endure before seeing him.

He diagnosed me with whooping cough and instructed Grandmother and Mother to take all the rugs off the floor and draperies off the windows at our house. He told them I had wet lungs and I couldn't lie down, even to sleep at night. It was because of those instructions that Grandma kept me up most nights and taught me the alphabet, multiplication, addition, reading, and writing.

I loved having Grandmother or Mother read me stories in the dining room, or Papa seat me on his lap to do math problems or build airplanes at the kitchen table with Brother and me.

Until September 1946, I had been homeschooled, although my grandmother didn't call it that or even know anything about that concept. Her objective at first was not to educate me especially for first grade, but to slow me down during the day and to keep me from coughing all night.

Because Mother had become a teacher by then, she was able to get grade-level books, and Grandma taught me with those. I loved the time with Grandma and the games we played. It didn't seem at all like schoolwork. Grandma would say, "You're going through this material lickety-split, girl. You seem to have a knack for this. I don't know where you are going with this, but you're going to give your first grade teacher a run for her money."

I had never been to a school except for Sunday school or visiting the Baptist College with Mother. I had never been away from home by myself for as long as a school day. Then, at age five and three quarters, I was registered for the first grade at Gibbs Elementary School.

Gibbs Elementary felt very similar to the Baptist

Mother Lois was a born teacher, always in the instructor's mode. She taught me the proper rules for reading and speaking, the French language, and how to sew. She had a funny sense of humor and liked to play tricks.

College, except the students were much younger at Gibbs. As I walked down the hall, I saw people sitting in rooms reading books and talking quietly together, doing math problems, or sitting in the library. There was active silence all around me. People tiptoed along the hallway, whispered to each other.

On that first school day, as I entered the small brightly lit first grade classroom, it was a whole new world of young brown people like me and friendly teachers. I was quite unaccustomed to being with so many people at one time.

No one seemed as frightened as I felt. They all behaved as though they were happy. "Take your seat and get out your pencil and notepad, and place your book bag beneath your desk," the teacher instructed. Grandma had provided me with a new notepad, a sharpened pencil, and color crayons, which I put on the desk.

The teacher wrote the date, September 18, 1946, on the chalkboard. She told us we would learn all names of the days of the week and the months of the year by heart and know how many days are in each month. Each day we would need to write the date on our pieces of paper along with our names.

I raised my hand at this point and said, "Mrs. Watson, I know mine already. Thirty days hath September, April, June, and November. All the rest have thirty-one, except February. It has twenty-eight, we find, unless it's leap year: Then it has twenty-nine."

She smiled slightly, but her voice was not friendly. "Oh, my! Tell me your name again."

"Melba Pattillo," I stuttered.

"Can you write your name?"

"I can print it. I'm learning to write it in cursive."

She stared at me and shook her head as she mumbled, "Uh-huh, is that so?"

Then she began to talk to the other children about the days of the week and the months of the year that I already knew. Right away I felt bored.

"Melba, you're not paying attention."

"Oh, yes I am. I want to learn new things," I shouted aloud.

"Are you certain you know all the days?" she asked.

"Yes, ma'am. Sunday, Monday, Tuesday, Wednesday, Thursday, Friday, Saturday, and then you start again. Six days you labor and then Sunday you worship God."

"Oh, my," she said.

The teacher seemed to me as though she was uncomfortable with me, and by the end of the week, the other children didn't like me either. Since the teacher said we were to be together for the rest of my elementary school year, it would become even more uncomfortable to me as time passed. No matter what the class was doing—writing names, learning numbers, doing math—if they were doing it today, I had already done it last year. I didn't want to do it all again. I wanted to move on. I misbehaved, becoming nervous and fidgety, daydreaming and moving around as I stared into space.

One day I was seated at my desk with my head down, doing my times tables (sixes, my favorite), when a lady walked into the classroom. She reminded me of my mother, as she had fair skin, freckles, and long brown hair.

"Come with me, Melba Joy," she said. "We are going to take you up to second grade."

During the months that I had been in the first grade class, I'd felt unwelcome. But that had started to slowly change with my fellow students. We knew one another's names, and I knew who liked me and who didn't. I was sad that I had to leave them now, even though the class was very boring. I had become accustomed to my desk and to people's faces. It was just before Christmas, and they would be having parties together. I didn't know where I was going or what I was going to do in the new classroom. Would the new people there know my name? Would they be nice to me?

Then the woman, Mrs. Aldridge, took me down the hallway and made a right turn into another classroom. This room was sunnier, with an entire line of windows to see outside. Some of these children were taller and bigger than I was; some were smiling. It sounded like I'd walked into a birthday party because the children were giggling so much. They had just had their snacks, so the room smelled of peanut butter, crackers, chips, and oranges. They had brightly colored crayons at their desks. A few wore saddle shoes just like mine. I had never been in a room full of so many people who were my color and my size.

"This is grade two, Melba. I'm Mrs. Osland," the teacher said. "We are going to see how you do here. Maybe you will like this better."

I felt tears rim my eyes. I wanted to cry. I had finally gotten comfortable and learned everybody's name in first grade. I didn't know if the second grade work would be too hard for me.

"May I go back now to my other class?"

"No, dear, you have to stay with me," said Mrs. Osland.

She pointed, and I looked at the other children in the room as I took the seat she'd indicated, near the window. When I turned to my right, so they wouldn't see my tears, I could see the trees and flowers outside. I put my book bag under my seat and scooted back in my chair. It was time to write another letter to God. I took out my tablet and began my letter. *Dear God, why are you being mean to me?*

"Please gather in your assigned reading circles," Mrs. Osland said, interrupting my letter. "Okay, Melba, come along, and we'll find the circle that fits for you."

I wondered what a reading circle was. Some children were seated in a ring at the front of the room with their chairs,

and they had some of the same books Grandma had me reading at home. Mrs. Osland had three books and said that she
would try me on each of them and see which one was best for
me. Then I would read with that group.

"Join us in reading aloud," she said.

I took my seat in the circle. Grandma had made me read
the book Mrs. Osland had once before. I was frightened to
read aloud, though. Suppose I messed up? The teacher seemed
astonished that I could read through the passages correctly
with speed. I read more than my share. Later, she told me
that book was for the highest group level, and I would have
to study what they had read in the past. But I explained I had
read that book a long time ago.

At lunchtime, I took my peanut butter and jelly sandwich
and carrots out of my brown bag. Two girls, who said their
names were Janice and Sadie, came over to say hello to me. I
took a deep breath and thought to myself, *Maybe this grade isn't
so bad after all.*

That was the beginning of my life outside my home. With
each class, I learned more about the huge world outside. I
loved reading and talking with the other students, finding out
who they were and where they came from. I wondered what
they thought about. Were they like me inside? Did they want
to get out of Little Rock, too?

From the first conversation at recess, though, I knew for
certain they had very different thoughts than mine. For one

thing, they didn't feel the same way about living in Little Rock or about the prison the white people had created for us. After I complained about everything that the white people had taken away from us, they just looked at me as though it was something they expected and were content with it. They had accepted the way the white people bossed us around. They had tolerated and learned to live with it. They were settling with that as though they couldn't do any better.

They did not hate or complain about living a separate life—not drinking out of a tattered water fountain marked colored, not being able to swim in the public pool or to ride on the good seats of the bus. They seemed not to know there were places where we could be free. They did not want to flag down the stork in order to get to another place. Two of my classmates said the stork did not deliver me and would not come back to pick me up. I couldn't believe my ears. I had waited a long, long time for Grandma and God to get me away. The stork was my only way out of here. I cried in the bathroom during the next recess. Why didn't they believe in my stork? What could I do now to be certain I would get away?

I had to go home and talk to Grandma. She would know. She would tell me what to do next. I couldn't stop crying even when we went back to the classroom after recess. The teacher sent me home early with a note in an envelope to give to my parents.

After she read it, Grandma and I had a long talk in the kitchen, sitting at the table as she peeled potatoes for dinner.

"It's up to you, child. Work hard, get your lesson, and trust God. You cannot wait on a stork. Wait on God."

"But it's taking too long," I screeched with anger.

"Patience! Have patience, or you will make yourself nuts. You can become really unhappy or you can go deep inside yourself and know God loves you as you do your personal best."

"Please, Grandma, since God has known you longer, He will listen to you," I said. "Tell Him I need to leave this place now, right now. Why don't you come with me?"

"Time will pass much faster if you get into your lesson book and make the best grades you can. Surprise your mother. Surprise me and surprise yourself. Go for all A's. Besides, when you trust God, He will give you peace and will answer your prayers in a much larger way than you'd hoped."

I took Grandma seriously. I dove into my books. When my teacher asked a question, I was the first to answer. I read as many books as I could get my hands on about all sorts of things. Mother cooperated by taking me to the Baptist College library. Slowly I grew to realize that therein lay the key to understanding all of the things I needed in order to escape the prison of Little Rock.

I was beginning to understand and define a new word: *segregation.*

# CHAPTER 9
## I'M NOT ALONE

**"PLEASE REPLACE THE NEWSPAPER PAGES** in order and fold it neatly," Grandma instructed me late one Thursday afternoon. "You won't be allowed to read it if you scatter pages about the room. There will be other people to read it after you."

That made me think about the fact that Papa read the paper every evening and that it always needed to be folded and placed on his chair. His chair was empty more and more, though. He was only with us part-time. Grandma and Mother continued to work very hard to keep secrets about whether Papa really had left home forever or whether or not he was on one of his frequent overnights.

*Maybe he will leave now but he will come back,* I always hoped. I didn't want to accept that maybe they might get a divorce.

Then Papa Will came home one evening to pack all of his belongings. I stood at the foot of the bed and watched him carefully arrange things in his suitcases. I watched him collect his guns from beneath his bed and put them in the new truck he had brought home, saying it was his new "toy."

"Papa, why are you leaving me?" I asked.

"I am not leaving you and Conrad, honey, but just trying a bit of life without your Mom."

"But why? Why do you have to live away from home? Why do this, and why now?" I was crying. He had left before for a Sunday and for a couple of nights. Conrad and I had just thought he was having overnights. Never had he packed all his belongings or taken his guns. I felt so unsafe knowing we wouldn't have him to protect us at night. What would we do if the Klan came to call us out?

"This has nothing to do with you and your brother," he said looking me directly in the eyes and holding my hands. "I still love the two of you—always that will be true."

"Yes, sir."

"And I still love your mother. But you can't live with every-one you love, and we can't live together."

I couldn't hold back my tears or my questions. "But why? Please say why!"

"Some things have no why, baby. They just are, that's all."

I stood on the front steps alone, waving goodbye to him. I knew this wasn't one of his overnights. My heart hurt, and my stomach was queasy. What would happen to us? He was so big and strong. Papa Will was called on by people targeted by the Klan, destined to be hanged. He was the one who had the strength, agility, and knowledge to get them safe passage out of town. He knew the routes and the transportation. People said he saved many lives.

After he drove away, I sat on the front steps waiting for Grandma to come home. Here was one more giant problem I had to talk to God about. *Help me please*, I prayed. *Help Papa come back.*

I spent more time alone pondering my life, reading my New World Encyclopedia, my dictionary, and my Bible. I felt as though I lived on a separate island and the rest of humanity lived on the mainland. I couldn't tell anyone all the secrets in my heart and in my head.

Time rushed past. Days all seemed like cookie-cutter copies of one another. It was April 1947, and I continued to seek private time with Grandma because she was the only one on this planet I felt close to. I could still ask her a few questions and enjoy watering the plants or listening to the radio with her. She was my best friend, my only real friend.

On one sunny afternoon when she had just returned from her church-ladies meeting, she rushed in to listen to our old broken radio. I noticed that she was very nervous that day.

Something exciting must have been about to happen, as she didn't take time to remove her Sunday-go-to-meeting dress as she would usually. Instead she had grabbed the radio and frantically worked to adjust it so we could hear what was going on.

On this day, she stood in front of the dining room cabinet and put the radio on the highest shelf she could reach, moving it around as she held a wire connected to it. The radio was sputtering and then we could hear the announcer explain about a man named Jackie Robinson—one of our folk playing with the Brooklyn Dodgers.

"The best baseball team ever," Grandma said.

Suddenly, I heard Grandma whisper the words, "Oh, my goodness." The crowd we heard on the radio in the big stadium was very angry, calling Mr. Robinson awful names and shouting, "Nigger, go home." I was frightened listening to them. What would they do to him? Would they hang him?

"That's the North. The man who put him on the team is white, not black. Our people are stronger there, and they have more power than they have here. They can make the law work on their side," Grandma assured me. "The policemen are more apt to rescue us up there. Some of them are even black. So the crowd won't be able to do very much. They can't hang him in broad daylight with the entire world listening on the radio and a stadium filled with Northern people watching."

I felt better hearing her assurances and comforted by the fact that our people were safer there than here. But the crowd's angry words hurt my feelings because they used some of the names I had been called.

"It's okay," Grandma said. "He's doing what he must in order to get all of us up and over the mountain."

"Why go where you're not welcome?" I asked.

"You cannot always go where others assign you to go forever, or you will never be free to claim anything as your own. When you're grown up, you get to make more choices because you can better protect yourself," Grandma told me. "He's doing that for a reason, Melba. He's moving our people up the mountain toward freedom. He's willing to do what it takes to get us over because he knows when he gets through, he'll take his brothers with him. If we are ever to have our freedom and get what we deserve, we must go where we are not welcome sometimes. The load is heavy, and the road is steep. We have to do what we need to do to climb up high enough to get over the mountain and claim our freedom."

From that day on, I knew that Grandma was doing the same thing. She had not given up just because she had curtsied to the white lady who screamed at her about her job. She was doing what was necessary to keep us moving up the mountain, doing what was necessary to keep us fed, safe, and alive.

Back in school, I could not focus on the work in class. My mind was whirling with thoughts of Mr. Robinson and his baseball and all those screaming people. Seeing him working so hard to move us forward made me realize I was not alone in my desire to have more freedom. I could not push down the excitement I felt on learning that I was not the only person on earth unhappy about how we were being treated by the white people. If Mr. Robinson was struggling and risking his safety for his equality, there must be many other people up North doing the same thing. I still couldn't figure out how or why white folks got their privileges and power automatically, even though we had to struggle and fight for ours, inch by inch by inch.

But it was a question I was determined to answer.

# CHAPTER 10
## BECOMING A REAL STUDENT

**SOMEHOW MR. ROBINSON'S STRUGGLE** to be a member of the baseball team lit my freedom candle. It signaled that I was filled with hope once more. Life seemed to move forward smoothly for almost a month. Yes, there was a reason to struggle for freedom, and it would come in God's time. We simply had to remain on guard and arm our warriors with strength and hope to prepare for the big battle still to come. Until then, we had to be ready to fight all the little battles we faced daily to stay alive.

At school, I began measuring time by my grade reports every six weeks and by the huge red X I would put on the calendar every day. It took a long time, but I stopped worrying so much about getting rid of the white people. I never gave up totally on being free and being equal, but rather each time white folks' shenanigans made me crazy, I tried to ignore that feeling and tuck it in the back of my mind. Instead of getting angry, I prayed for understanding. I told myself that this was today and by tomorrow our lives were all going to be so much better.

Summer came, the flowers bloomed, and the sun stayed out longer as the school semester came to an end. With school out, there was so much extra time and nothing to do, with only Conrad and Grandma around. Grandma had quit her day job to be with us, so I spent a lot of time helping her in the garden. Summers were lonely, though, with only Sunday school and vacation Bible school to attend and not a lot of friends around otherwise.

Mother attempted to keep us busy. We were directed to read a book a week and write a book report to be delivered to her verbally each Friday. Mother spent her time in school during the summer taking graduate-level courses.

Grandma's solution to keeping us busy was setting up what she called a House Systems Program. She said, "You can never get away with not being able to take care of yourselves." She slowly taught us to iron, wash clothes, and take care of the house by dusting, sweeping floors, and watering the more than one hundred indoor plants she kept. We also learned to cook and how to stretch the food budget. I liked baking gingerbread cookies best. Conrad's favorite to bake was butter cookies.

One summer she had us create our own gardens. I planted tomatoes, lettuce, peas, and collard greens in my garden. "Great, child, you've been watching me!" Grandma said, folding her apron over her arm.

There was a whole group of women who shared their seeds with us, so we had many good choices. She taught us to sew and to knit and crochet. There were quilting sessions with Grandma's friends. She said that there was no reason why men shouldn't be proficient at these chores, so Conrad learned everything I did.

The summer did drag on, and we were very chipper when it came to an end. Back at school, more and more people were becoming my friends. The more I kept my complaints about how white people treated us to myself, the more my social life improved. The small group of my friends seemed to have the same goals: to behave appropriately and make good grades. I valued my membership in that group and received adult approval daily.

There was little talk these days of our rights being taken away and no talk of how we went to separate schools, even though we had only old, torn books; typewriters with broken keys; and tables with three legs carted over from the white school every September, as though we were the junkyard. There was only talk of what white people wanted and how they expected us to behave. It was as though we were studying their requests, even at school, for we certainly didn't want to upset any of them. This was not the first time in my young life that I had done so.

Even so, I was desperate to find out where the many, many rules that they controlled us with came from. Were they in a book issued from heaven? Who got to make the rules up, and how did you add to them or take away from them? If God really loved us equally, where was our rulebook for them? I stopped talking to Grandma about my dissatisfaction with white people and their rules. Instead I wanted to review and memorize all the rules so I could obey them and avoid confrontations, because I didn't want to be carted away forever or killed like Mr. Harvey. If that happened, I would have lived my entire life under the unfair and unequal rules that white people created. Before death, I told myself, I would get to enjoy just one day of being equal and feeling equal. That was the hope I held on to, no matter what.

As time passed, I grew more mature and more aware of the sacrifice it had taken for my people to live and grow up in the South all those many years before me. I began to read more of the history of my people. I often felt disappointed in my own "good girl" behavior, but I didn't know what else to do in order to help us move further ahead. I spent hours trying to figure out what I must do to rescue myself while not endangering my family or anyone around me.

I threw my interest and energy into school and homework. I remained an outsider, with just a small handful of friends, never invited to join the popular party kids in their very exclusive groups. At first my feelings were hurt. I was left out of the Maypole dance because the teacher said I was a head taller than most of the boys in the class. The same thing happened with the Broadway dance show and every group performance being planned. Her excuse was always that my early body development made me look older than the rest of the class. So I became accustomed to the fact that I would be left behind. But when exam results were read aloud, I knew for certain I would never be left behind. I worked hard to ensure that I would always earn A's.

During the summer when I was eight, my family went by train to Saint Louis to see some of our cousins. The porters brought us food from the dining car because we couldn't go through the white-occupied cars to the dining room. Everything was separated on that train. We only briefly saw anybody white on the train. Sometimes a porter walked through the car with a real, hot meal that was being served in the dining car. That made me realize that there on the train as well, we were not being treated as equals. We had cold sandwiches, ate at our seats. Why didn't we deserve hot dishes?

When we reached Saint Louis, we saw that there was some freedom for our people. It was exciting not to see those horrid WHITE ONLY signs anywhere. There were restaurants with nice sections for us. People in Saint Louis seemed to accept us and never called us names. We didn't have to step off the sidewalks for them. Our people didn't seem afraid. As evening approached, they left their lights on, kept the shades open, and sat on their porches. There were even clubs and bars where both white and black people went together. In Saint Louis, we didn't feel the white people were smothering us, circling all around, telling us what to do.

I got to ride on a merry-go-round for the first time, and nobody stared. Everybody smiled. I wanted to get my favorite things, a peppermint stick and a dill pickle. Momma gave me the money, and I could pay for them myself. When I went to the store to get them, no one pushed me out of line for anyone else. The store clerk even talked to me and took the money right out of my hand. Here, for the first time, I found that I could live a different way. The Little Rock feeling of fear was gone after two days.

It seared my heart and soul when we had to go back to Little Rock again. Getting on the train, I felt this heavy shadow come over me. It was like a curtain had been lowered in front of me, covering my soul. The closer we got to Little Rock, the more I saw my mother and grandmother losing their power as adults, acting more like children or humble servants.

The only bright spot on our return to Little Rock was passing my father out in a vast field of train cars. He was dressed in his coveralls and working at his job. Conrad and I thought it was a nice surprise, and we were happy to see him. Then, we became sad yet again when we remembered he wouldn't be at home when we got there, and we weren't seeing him very often anymore.

When the train pulled into Little Rock, we were separated from the white people again. We had our own exit door from the train, no porters to help us, as they were busy with the white passengers, and once again the separate, dreary waiting room to go through as we left the station.

Saint Louis had been like a trip to paradise. I really wanted out of Little Rock, but Mother said we were there among family and friends, with jobs, and it would be too difficult to move us as a family. Little Rock was what she knew, where she was comfortable.

It was good being back at school with friends and lots of work to occupy my mind. Schoolwork was my escape. I kept myself busy so I wouldn't think too much about Little Rock or about the dream of leaving there.

The first weeks of school passed quickly with lots of homework and chores. The studies were different with the new school year, and the teachers' expectations of me were different. Like a whirlwind, time passed, and it was Thanksgiving, with the aroma of turkey and Grandma's baking filling the house. Then before I knew it, I was looking forward to my birthday in December. I was expecting God to do something special on this birthday.

# CHAPTER 11
## THE WORLD IS MY BIRTHDAY GIFT

**ON DECEMBER 7, 1950,** I was going to put all battles aside and celebrate my birthday. But there was a different kind of struggle waiting for me: the lack of gifts. Most everybody said, "Wait till Christmas. It's only eighteen days to wait. Santa's got big gifts—big enough for your birthday and your Christmas!"

I wanted to shout, "I'd rather have two small gifts and one of them today on my birthday!" I also dreamed of having my own birthday party. If I could have one, maybe friends would all bring me gifts as well. But mother said it would have to happen after she was finished taking graduate degree courses at the University of Arkansas. She didn't have the time or the money to give me such a party, because the classes and books were so expensive.

She said she had to concentrate on doing her best because she was one of the first of our women given permission to register for classes in that white university. If she made high grades, then others might be invited to enter. Being at that university brought opportunity for a better job and better life for us all. When I complained, she told me I would have to understand that her education would bring us better gifts than money could buy. So I celebrated my birthday just with my family.

I was nine years old, and I was very worried that my father wouldn't attend. By then, Papa Will and Mother Lois were talking about getting a divorce. I couldn't stop myself from thinking about what might happen when they got divorced. Would we still be a family? Would he forget my birthday? How often would he have dinner with us or let us sit on his lap to do a puzzle?

I was certain Grandma India would never forget about my special day. She was different. I could count on her. I knew she would do something to make me feel happy, and I couldn't wait to see what it was.

A neighbor dropped me off after school to wait for Grandma to come home from work, so my birthday celebration could begin. Mother Lois was still at school, and my little brother was playing next door with his friend, Harold.

So, I waited in our big house, all alone. But I was too excited to be afraid.

As I waited for Grandma, I found myself looking at the big brown leather chair in the living room where my Papa Will always used to sit reading the evening newspaper and doing his crossword puzzles. How I missed seeing him there.

I stood up and moved slowly about the living room, running my fingers along the shiny black radio with its brass knobs. That radio was like a family member. Each Sunday night we would all gather around it to listen to *Fibber Mc-Gee and Molly* and *Amos 'n Andy*, funny shows that made us all laugh.

Just then, Grandma's key in the front door jolted my daydreaming. I rushed to see her. She was struggling against the cold, gray winter wind, carrying a huge round ball in her arms. What could it be? Maybe it was a plump frozen goose? Or was it a Tiffany lamp she had found on a junk pile? She walked into the dining room and set the big ball down on the table.

Removing her gloves, she walked over to the kitchen stove to warm up her hands in its low flame. When her hands were warm, she took off her coat and turned to me with a smile. Was she hiding some mysterious secret?

"This is your birthday surprise," she whispered, smiling. "Happy birthday, my angel warrior. Happy birthday!" She invited me into her arms for a warm hug.

"What is it, Grandma? Tell me, tell me!" I thought I would burst with excitement before she could get the words out.

"I'm giving you the world for your birthday," she said. Then she added, "Because you deserve it." Sparkles of joy exploded in my chest. What could she mean, the world? I didn't understand, but I trusted her to give me something special.

As she uncovered a globe, I couldn't believe my eyes. I had never seen an actual world globe this big up close and personal, much less had one of my own. I had seen them in the library, of course. Even though I could see it was a little tattered, mine was so beautiful because it was mine. The surface was puckered and flaking, with all of its many colors beginning to blend. It resembled some of the other throw-away things she brought home from the discarded piles outside white ladies' houses where she cleaned or the hotel where she worked as a maid. But I didn't care that it was a hand-me-down. I knew Grandma could make magic. She would make it like brand-new.

I looked closely to find my favorite city, San Francisco, California. I knew a lot about that city because our friend Steven lived there and came to visit his family, who lived next door to us, every summer. He always came with lots of talk about new things that made my candle of hope burn brighter. He said that in California white folks were not in charge of our people as they were here in Arkansas. In California, people like us could even attend the beautiful schools that

white people also attended without threats and ugliness. Oh, how I wished I could go to California. Grandma came back and rubbed her hands across the surface of the globe, interrupting my dreams of that magical place.

"We'll need lots of baking soda to help with the cleaning. Come on with me to the store," she said.

"No. No, Grandma, please, not on my birthday. I don't want to." I still hated going to the grocery store. I didn't want the mean white people there to treat me like I didn't count on my birthday.

"Oh, what's all this complaining, now? Get your coat and walk with me."

I knew it wasn't any use trying to talk my way out of it, so I pulled my heavy green woolen coat with the hood that Grandma had made for me off the rack. We walked out the front door, to face the chill air and a thick glaze of ice under our feet. I held Grandma's arm even more tightly.

We walked the two blocks to the store, stepping carefully trying to avoid the patches of ice, looking down, trying not to skid into a fall. As we reached the store, what little sun there had been that day was setting and the sky blended into the gray haze that swallowed everything around us.

Grandma pulled open the heavy wooden door to the store, and we stepped inside. Wondrous aromas of potatoes, onions, smoked meat, and spices mixed to warm our faces and tease our nostrils. We walked directly over to the brightly colored sacks of flour, and Grandma reached above them to the stacked boxes of baking soda.

"Aintie." The voice jarred my ear. She wasn't their aunt.

"Aintie," I heard someone say once more, "you gotta get new glasses. I hope you're not thinking of reaching in front of me."

Suddenly, there was a white man standing right in front of us, scowling at Grandma. She quickly pulled her hand back to her side and said she was

Even though I pleaded not to go to the store because it was my birthday, I knew that Grandma always got her way. So I gave in.

sorry. I looked at her. Why should she be sorry? Wasn't he the one who had stepped in front of her? But I knew not to say a word. Grandma had a look of fear on her face. She stepped back, bumping into the rack of bread and cakes, and grabbed my hand to pull me to her.

The man rolled his eyes at us and said, "Careful, now. You niggers better keep in mind where your place is." Then he walked on.

I looked up to see her face, and Grandma dug a smile from beneath her layers of frowns and sadness. "Okay, let's try again." She looked down at me and reached up and grasped the orange box of Arm & Hammer baking soda in defiance, being sure neither the clerk nor the cashier saw her. She would show the clerk by the cash register the box when she paid for it, and he would never know she'd taken it off the shelf herself. Then she took my hand and we moved toward the meat counter. "I might as well get some ham hocks for the collard greens and a chicken. After all, it is your birthday. Let's spoil ourselves."

I struggled to show her my brave face, but I wanted to run out the front door right then. I knew what always happened at the meat counter. We would be forced to step out of line and let the white people in front of us.

We waited and waited in line. Just when the clerk looked over the top of the counter and said, "Aintie, what you gonna have today? You need some neck bone scraps?"

"No, sir, I want—" In the middle of Grandma's sentence, a white lady stepped in front of her and the clerk said, "Oh, Mrs. Dawson, I didn't see you coming there. Aintie is a good negra. She'll be glad to step back and let me take care of y'all first."

I wanted Grandma to say, *Don't call me* negra. *You know very well it sounds like* nigger. I wanted her to say, *No! No! I won't step back. It's my turn, fair and square.*

But she didn't. She stepped back, and we kept on waiting. I thought to myself, *We'll miss my birthday if we have to wait much*

THE WORLD IS MY BIRTHDAY GIFT

*longer.* Besides, I couldn't help wanting to say, *What place? Who says we have a place? Where is it?*

Then once again, after all the white people were served and we'd finally gotten to our turn, suddenly the butcher called for a woman named Mrs. Wishart to step in front of us. "Come right ahead, Mrs. Wishart. I didn't see you standing there. As I've always said, Aintie India is a good negra. She'll let you go first."

Afraid we'd be late for my birthday, I couldn't help shouting out loud, "No!"

Grandma India quickly said, "Shush."

The clerk had already begun to lift his hand to hit me when a voice from behind us said, "No, no, India is helping with my list, let her go ahead."

I was crouching down to avoid the fist of the butcher, but was so happy to hear the voice of Mrs. Wishart letting us go first. Grandma had worked for her a few years back, before her husband died.

We collected our things and went to the back of the line of people waiting at the counter to pay. One time, two times, three times, and four, just as our turn came, a white lady rushed up and jumped in front of us, saying it was her dinnertime and she had to hurry.

I whispered to Grandma that I wanted her to stick out her foot and trip them so they'd fall. But she whispered back, saying that was un-Christian-like behavior and that God was watching. Still, I thought, *I bet this would never happen in California.*

Just as I was thinking of what it would be like to burn the store down, Mrs. Wishart came up behind us, and when the clerk looked at us to get us to move aside for her, she said, "Oh, no, they are with me."

She added her purchases to ours and paid for it all. Grandma always said Mrs. Wishart was a different sort of white lady. "A kind one, who looked me in the eyes," Grandma said. We collected our things and walked out. I was so frightened we'd get caught because Grandma no longer worked for her.

But when we got outside, the three of us huddled as though we belonged together in order to keep folks who might be watching from telling on us. Grandma thanked Mrs. Wishart, who told me to have a nice birthday and a wonderful evening. She had given me the best gift ever. She'd given me back my birthday celebration.

I explained to Grandma how surprised I was.

Grandma said, "God didn't give all the white people white sheets and crosses. He gave some of them angel wings."

On the way home, both Grandma and I were silent for the first block. But then I couldn't hold myself in any longer. Mrs. Wishart was kind, but no one else at the store was. "Why do you let them say those things to us?" I asked.

"White folks can't help their ignorance. And it's our task

to learn to cope with it, if we want to stay alive and keep our peace of mind."

"But I don't understand," I said, even though I was always trying to.

"You'll understand later. For now, you have to trust me and trust God." Grandma had a real faith in God. She had always gone to church at least three nights a week and on Sundays. She talked to God like a real friend, and taught me to talk to Him, too, in prayer and even by writing letters to Him sometimes.

"Just write another letter to God," she whispered.

But God felt very far away, and I already had a stack of letters to God that I'd written ever since I was four years old.

"I don't want to understand later," I told her. "I want them to stop bothering us now. I want them to treat us like they treat their people. I don't ever want to be treated like that when I grow up."

"I know how you feel, child. But it's your birthday. Let's say out loud, for God to hear, a list of all the things you want to be true by the time your next birthday rolls around in 1951."

I thought about my list. It had been the same last year. I told her I wanted to be able to go to the movies, ride in the front of the bus, eat lunch at five-and-dime, and to have all the people who spoke to us the way they did in that store apologize. Plus, I wanted to be able to ride the merry-go-round and swim in Fair Park Pool and to try on clothes in the department stores downtown.

As we unlocked the front of our home and crossed into the hallway, Grandma said, "It seems to me you'll need to write two letters to God. The first must be all the things you're grateful for. The second one should list all your wants, needs, and desires."

I began my letter of gratitude to God even before the party started.

# CHAPTER 12
## HOPE THAT THE WORLD CAN BE MINE

**THE JOY OF MRS. WISHART'S** sweet deed lingered in my heart for the entire evening because she had given me a birthday gift that consisted of a promise: a promise that white people could treat us as though we were human if the circumstances were right. So, my heart was filled with hope. And when I looked at my globe, my heart was nearly exploding.

After we put our coats away and warmed our hands, Grandma quickly washed the chicken, stuck an orange inside, rubbed it with butter, added onions and garlic to the pan, and popped it into the oven. Then she added the ham hocks to a big pot of boiling water spiced with garlic, celery, and onion. All those delicious goodies would cook that way for a time and then she would add the meat to the collard greens left over from last night's dinner. This would be their second day of cooking. Two-day-old collard greens were the best. I was starting to get hungry just watching her stir the pot. When Grandma put the lid on and turned the burner down low, we sat down with the baking soda, vinegar, and water to begin cleaning the globe.

Grandma began pulling on her cotton work gloves and mixing the baking soda we'd got at the store with the vinegar and water. With this cleaning potion, she could make things come alive with color and shine. I had seen her do it so many times with tattered books and soiled toys. I could always tell when she got it just the way she wanted because she would give me a big smile and a big hug.

How I loved to sit and watch the way she worked. I wanted to grow up to become just like Grandma India, because she was always so certain she could do a good job. She said that joy and confidence came from totally trusting in God and trusting in yourself to have the skills you needed at hand. I also liked the way she always looked fresh and tidy. Her housedress was always crisply starched. Her long, shiny hair, with its gray strands here and there, was tucked into a neatly pinned bun at the nape of her neck. As I leaned in close to her, I could smell the dab of vanilla extract she put at the back of her ear for her special perfume.

Grandma India ever so carefully scrubbed off the globe.

It seemed as if we sat there forever. Every now and then, she held the globe close, peering through her magnifying glass at portions of it. She stopped only once to get up and add the ham hocks to the collard greens, and then their aroma took over the house. I knew her freshly baked cornbread would soon be casting its spell as well. I could feel the celebration only moments away. Excitement was building inside my chest like a sunburst. I hoped the other dinner guests would come soon.

Conrad stormed through the door, laughing and shouting and bothering us, babbling so fast that some of his words were garbled. He wanted to know what we were doing. He glared at my globe and walked toward it. My heart pounded.

Just then Grandma shouted, "It's almost six o'clock, boy. Go on to the bathroom and start your bath."

He stopped pestering us and went away singing "Old MacDonald Had a Farm" in his silliest voice. I was glad he was out of the room because I wanted to be alone with Grandma and the globe.

I started to talk to her, to finally unburden my heart of some of the things I'd been fretting about. I explained that I was worried that my mother wouldn't come home in time to celebrate my birthday. This was one of her late nights taking class over at the white folks' university. She worked so hard, teaching all day, then studying at night for her master's degree. I knew she was one of only a few of our people allowed to attend that university. I wondered if she was frightened mixing with all those people who didn't want her there.

While I told Grandma that I was worried that Mother Lois wouldn't come home in time to sing "Happy Birthday," what I didn't say was that I was afraid my father wouldn't be there at all. But sometimes it was almost as if Grandma could read my mind.

"Your papa will surely come for a visit tonight," she said as she took her pen knife and scraped the base of the globe. Then she looked at me as though waiting to hear my thoughts about his absence. But instead, I kept my thoughts to myself.

My then-daily letters to God had not been answered when it came to Papa, and I could not say my wish aloud, because I was keeping it quiet, hoping the Lord would soon understand how important it was to me. My secret hope was just as strong as ever, though: I wanted us to become a family again.

"We'd better get this globe done quickly so we can clean up and be ready to finish dinner," Grandma said as if knowing I couldn't talk about it. "Company will be arriving soon."

Before long, Grandma dried off the globe. Then she took out her glue and showed me the envelope where she'd put the pieces of countries and oceans and mountains that had broken off. She began very carefully to paste them back onto the surface. There was a period of silence between us as Grandma India worked on the globe. The only sound in the room was our breathing.

Then she said, "There, there, child. Now you can get a glimpse at the rest of the world."

Suddenly, Grandma India took a deep breath and stood up tall, rubbing her hands against her apron pockets. She had done it once again—she had made magic. To me, the globe looked just like new. I reached up to stretch my arms partway around her waist and hugged her as tight as I could.

I looked at all those places painted on my beautiful globe. Maybe one day I could travel to a city where the grocery stores would welcome me and let me take my place in line without having white people jumping in front of me or calling my grandma names.

I studied the globe and started to spin it round and round with my fingertips. I found the United States, Arkansas, and then Little Rock, where I lived. Little Rock was in the middle of the United States of America. It felt to me like it was down at the bottom of a deep salad bowl. The sides were tall and they cut you off from everything else. I wanted more than anything to get to the edge of that country-size bowl, where the air must be clean and fresh. I imagined if I lived someplace on the very edge of the continent, like California, that the wonderful ocean breeze would set me free.

Suddenly the doorbell rang, bringing me back to my birthday party. "It must be our *rellies*," Grandma said pointing to the front door. "Well, let's go."

My relatives arrived for my party, hustling in the door,

removing their coats, and hugging me. I knew exactly what would happen next: They would focus all their attention on me. It would be fun at first, but I knew they wouldn't be giving me a gift until Christmas.

"Well, Missy Melba, I'd only come out in this weather after a long day's work for you, child," said Auntie Mae. "I'm your gigantic present."

It was the same each year with Auntie Mae—excuses and hugs, but no gift.

Her daughter, my grown-up cousin, Fuchsia, would always say, "If only I wasn't in school, I would buy you the biggest dolly."

Uncle Charlie and Aunt Annie would always follow the first two, carrying large bowls or huge metal pans of piping hot, spirit-lifting food. I couldn't fault them for bringing what delighted everyone, and certainly I was grateful. Behind them came Uncle Morris, who had the best smile and gold teeth.

Soon, it was almost six thirty; it was getting late, and dinner was ready, but Mother and Papa Will hadn't arrived for my birthday celebration. As I sat down at the dining room table with the green linen napkins, used only on special occasions, the doorbell rang again. It rang so hard and long that Grandma India came running out of the kitchen.

"Shhhhhhhh," she said, motioning to me. "Be quiet."

It was dark outside now, and supper was ready. Who

could it be? The only people we were expecting were Mother Lois and Papa Will, and they had a key to the door. Could this bell ring be a trick?

"Who is it?" shouted Conrad as he raced from his bedroom, pulling on the left arm of his bathrobe. "I'll get it!"

"Do you want to go to bed with no dinner?" Grandma whispered fiercely. "Get back there and be quiet, boy."

Grandma shoved him toward his room. I could see in her face that she was frightened. What if it was the Klan? What if they had come to get us because they didn't like Mother going to their school? They had threatened in the past to do something to keep her away.

Once again I was surrounded by a whole room of adults who were silent and shaken by the possible arrival of the Klan. I was thinking, *Why isn't somebody preparing to fight back if it is the Klan?*

But I also knew that this was what we feared each and every night: the ride of the Klan. One neighbor recently had been hauled out of his house in the middle of the night by the Ku Klux Klan.

Then a familiar voice filled my ears. "It's me," Papa Will cried through the door. "Come on and open up. Everything's all right. But hurry! Open up."

Grandma India's forehead relaxed, and she heaved a sigh of relief. The wrinkles in her face turned into smile lines. "Coming, Will! Coming!"

As she unlatched the chain, Papa Will's huge six-foot-four-inch-tall frame lurched forward into the room. Lashed to his back with a rope was a large square box. I couldn't tell what it was, but it looked very heavy. Even in the freezing December night, beads of perspiration rolled off Papa Will's forehead. He grunted as he stumbled inside.

Conrad, barefoot but wearing his green-striped bathrobe and jumping up and down like a frisky puppy, chased close behind Papa into the living room. I followed right after them both. But then I couldn't help turning back to see what Grandma was thinking.

Her eyes were full of questions and surprise. Shutting the door and locking it behind her, Grandma stood a few steps back. What on earth could Papa Will have brought? And what made him think it would be allowed in the living room? He knew very well how particular Grandma India and Mother were about that precious room.

"Television!" Papa Will boomed out as he lowered the big box down to the floor. He wiped his brow with the back of his hand. "Whew, that was a mite heavier than I'd expected." He stood back and grinned proudly. Then we could see there on the front of the box was a picture of a television set.

"Television?" Grandma said, as if she couldn't believe her eyes.

"Television!" Conrad screamed, bursting with excitement.

"Television," I whispered. We had never been allowed to

watch television at anyone else's house. Not even one program. I had walked past television sets in the stores and wanted so badly to look up close or touch, but I knew better.

"Well, Will Pattillo," Grandma said, "how do you go about turning it on?"

"Let's see." Papa took a box knife out of his pocket and cut the cardboard, then he lifted the most wonderful sight I'd ever seen out of the box. He crawled around the television, putting on his brown horn-rimmed glasses to read tags, then taking them off to see what was written on the back of the cabinet. He tinkered with the box for what seemed forever as the black-and-white patterns zigzagged across the screen. Uncle Morris and Uncle Charlie stood in the corner shouting information about what to do next, even though they didn't have televisions themselves.

Finally, Grandma India ordered us all to come to the dining room. It was seven o'clock. We still had to have my party, and my brother had to get to bed by eight and I by nine—though maybe because this was a celebration, we would get to stay up later. We sat down at the dinner table, but I was really sad that Mother Lois hadn't gotten home in time for dinner.

As Grandma India was scooping up the collard greens onto our plates and Papa was cutting the chicken and cornbread, I heard the front door open and Mother called out to us. "Hello, family, where's the birthday girl?"

"In here!" we all shouted.

"Hurry!" I motioned Conrad to move over a seat so Papa and Mother could sit beside each other.

"Why?" Conrad asked. "Mama can sit over there."

Then Papa told Mama that he had a surprise for her. "It's in honor of Melba's birthday," he said, "and it's really for everyone." She looked up at him with a girlish grin, and we could all see how much he was taken with her. I hoped once again that this might be the beginning of our new family life.

When all our plates were clean and our stomachs were filled, Grandma told us to turn out the lights, and she brought the beautifully decorated ginger cake to the table with candles blazing. "Make a wish," she said.

I closed my eyes and wished I could go to California and then I huffed and puffed, trying to blow out every single candle. Then they all sang "Happy Birthday" to me. I felt so happy, even though Mother Lois gave me the usual speech about how I would have a wonderful big Christmas gift to make up for there being no birthday present.

After dessert, Papa Will told Mother Lois to come and look at the surprise. We all rushed back into the living room. There, Papa tinkered with the television knobs until it lit up. Then, right before our eyes, real people were talking and singing and dancing in our own living room. A man in a tuxedo came up on the screen and started telling jokes.

We crowded into that room with the aroma of the food still surrounding us, some people still munching on their drumsticks. Conrad and I just sat on the floor and stared. Mother and Papa Will sat on the couch looking straight ahead at the picture in silence. Grandma India's eyes were as wide as saucers, and her mouth was open. None of us spoke for such a long time. I almost wet my pants because I didn't want to leave the television to go to the bathroom.

My relatives all declared their feelings about the set from their astonishment at live people dancing in the living room, to *we need to get one or come to your house every night.*

My grandma told them all, "I don't think so."

*Thank God tomorrow is Saturday,* I thought to myself. *All I'm gonna do is watch television. That'll make Saturday wonderful.* Then— whack!

Suddenly, the television screen went black, leaving the room in darkness. Grandma India had pulled the plug on our great surprise, and she turned on the lights.

"This TV is the devil incarnate," she said in a loud voice. "It will eat away at our minds. You'll become like tree trunks."

We all stared at her.

"I've seen it in some of those homes I worked in. Television gets the best of the family love. People stop talking to each other," she said. "None of them move or do crafts or projects. No one spends time with the Lord."

On and on she went, pacing back and forth and waving her arms in the air. She said we had to schedule television and not let it schedule us. We could never watch television without an adult in the room, she said. Then she announced it was time for us kids to help clear the table and do our story reading and head for bed.

Any other day, I would have been upset to have her turn off the television like that and just send us to bed. But tonight, in my room, my globe was waiting for me. Tonight, on my ninth birthday, I wanted to go to my room and explore my globe. I wanted to fuel my dreams. I wanted to enjoy my gift of the world.

# CHAPTER 13
## BLESSED

*ON FRIDAY EVENING, A WEEK* after my ninth birthday, Mother Lois laid down the law and drew up a new set of rules. She declared a television diet. We could have only a total of two hours during the week, and two hours on the weekend. We had to sign up on paper and tell her which programs we wanted to watch, why, and how it would contribute to our education.

By noon the next day, in order to keep us from watching our television, Grandma ushered us to the car. "We need to get going on Christmas."

Riding in our two-door 1949 navy blue Chevy with the slant back, we started by singing, "She'll Be Coming Around the Mountain When She Comes." Conrad and I had to admit to each other that it was much more fun to go with Grandma and Mother Lois downtown than to sit at home watching TV.

During the short fifteen-minute ride, we talked to each other and pointed out the new buildings being constructed. We counted different kinds of funny-looking cars and laughed at people and their pets walking along the streets. We asked Grandma and Mother Lois, "What makes the clouds look like puffy balls of cotton, and what makes the sky always blue? Does God live above the clouds?"

Grandma said, "You know that. God lives above the clouds."

Mother Lois then said, "God is able to take the different gases from other planets and mix them to make the sky blue. You remember we told you there are other planets?"

But the nearer we drew to downtown, the more I felt that familiar, frightening quiver like Jell-O in my stomach. We would be surrounded and smothered by white people and their rules as I saw those signs that made me feel sad. Everything was marked COLORED or WHITE, to prove who was in charge. I read COLOREDS MUST STAND BEHIND THIS LINE, and at a laundry, a sign said, WE DO NOT WASH COLORED FOLKS' CLOTHES HERE. Signs reading NEGRAS NOT WELCOME, WE DO NOT SERVE COLOREDS, or NO COLOREDS IN THIS AREA AFTER 6:00 P.M. were tacked up all over.

It frightened me, as always, when some of the white faces

glared at us as we drove past. It seemed like they were silently saying, "I'm better than you, and I'm gonna make you do what I want." Sometimes they would sneer outright, for no reason, before I looked down to avoid eye contact.

"We have to mind our p's and q's," Grandma reminded us.

Conrad and I always wondered what those "p's and q's" actually were. Politeness and quietness?

It was as though the list of what I could and could not do was printed in a strange place in my mind. One by one, the list clicked out as though a white master were typing it. Don't look white people in the eye; don't do things to get their attention; don't touch anything; don't say anything unless spoken to; and then, mind your manners. Don't smile and don't talk too loud. Walk with dignity and pride, but never, never walk in front of one of them or cross their path. Wait until they pass. I clenched my teeth and my fists, but I didn't say a word of complaint because I knew it was no use.

Mother Lois parked our car, and we began walking to the heart of downtown Little Rock toward the department stores. My heart was beating so fast, I could hear it like a drum in my ears. I wanted to turn and run back to my own neighborhood, where people would welcome us and where I felt safe at least some of the time. As we walked, I held Grandma India's hand very tight. It had been icy that morning, but the sun had come out, softening the ground ice into mush. Still, the dampness and the bite of the cold ate at my bones, and I had lost my mittens. I hoped I would get another pair in my Christmas stocking. I knew better than to think I could try any on in the white people's stores.

I tried to look down at the ground as we walked and to avoid having to look a white person in the eye. Before we got to the first store, I had muddied my shoes three times stepping off the curb to let white people pass. Hot, angry prickles rose in my chest. As usual, I was so disappointed in Mother and Grandmother for not standing up and saying something as the white people waited, expecting us to give in and step off the sidewalk. When I had asked once before why we couldn't stand up for ourselves, Mother Lois had blurted out with anger, "You have no idea what you're saying, girl. To do that would mean risking our lives and limbs."

I knew the rules were there to keep us alive and protect us. On the other hand, I thought there were enough of my people to do something about getting our rights and gaining respect. A sour-lemon feeling grew inside my stomach, and an unhappiness that wouldn't go away. I asked Grandma once more when God would make it our turn to stay on the sidewalk and touch what we wanted to in the store.

She told me I had more letter writing and praying to do.

"Pooh," I whispered. "Pooh, pooh, pooh."

By the time we got to the stores, those old Little Rock feelings had risen up inside of me again. Bright red and green lights and Santa figures surrounded us, but they weren't for me.

Mother Lois reminded us, "Put your hands in your pockets, children. You know better than to touch anything." I began steaming inside with frustration as I looked around and saw all the white children touching and picking up and trying on. One girl even dropped a beautiful knit scarf on the floor, but her mother didn't chide her like my mother was chiding me.

"We'll just have a feast looking. We may not be able to touch, but thank God, we can look all we want," Grandma said in a low voice.

So, we looked. On both floors and down narrow aisles we walked amid tables of all the things I wanted to call my own. Raggedy Ann dolls and dollhouses, little aluminum dishes to play kitchen. And things for dress-up: furry collars, crinoline slips, rose-smelling toilet water, bracelets, and new saddle shoes.

As we made our way back down to the first floor and the door leading out to the street, Conrad got very angry because he wanted to sit on Santa's lap. How could we explain to him what he already knew deep down inside, but could not accept? The store's Santa was for white people. And they thought Conrad wasn't good enough to deserve that Santa.

So we stood for an instant and stared at the line of white children waiting for their turn with Santa. Tears seeped from

Conrad's eyes, washing away his dimpled smile. His face took on the sad veil of someone trying to get used to sacrificing what he wanted so badly.

"Didn't that Santa bring toys to all the children?" he asked. If so, he wondered, why couldn't he sit on his lap now?

As we moved on, I could smell the aroma of hot food coming from the lunch counter. It was now almost three thirty in the afternoon, and it would have been nice to have a Grapette soda and bite of hot dog. I kept my mouth shut about my wants, though, because I knew what the answer would be. All the restaurants had signs saying they would not serve us. There was never a place we could eat downtown. Never, never, *never*.

"I brought a snack in the car," Grandma said, taking my arm as if she had read my mind and understood my disappointment. *Just be grateful,* I thought.

But by then, I also had to go to the restroom, and so did the others. It was always nerve-racking when we had to go to the bathroom, because we all knew there was never a restroom nearby with COLORED marked on the door. I walked ahead of my family past the first floor where the walls were clean and white, and the doors to the women's bathroom were yellow with daisies on it. I paused for a moment and leaned against a wooden column, but I knew very well that I couldn't go inside that door.

"Don't even think about it." Grandma nuzzled me in the back of the neck with her thumb.

"No, ma'am," I said, but I felt something inside me rile up.

"I mean it, Melba Joy," she said. "Don't let your mind drift to things you can't do or have. Instead be grateful for things you can do."

I walked way ahead of her so she wouldn't see my sour face and got lost once again in my own thoughts until Grandma's voice brought me up sharply. I had to go to the bathroom so very badly.

"You're nine years old now. A young lady. You can hold yourself in." She sounded a little worried. "If you have to go, you have to use our restrooms," she added.

Grandma didn't know it, but she had nothing to worry about. I wasn't going to break that rule again. I knew too well that bad things would happen if I violated the white people's rules. How sad that made me feel. I must have written to God twenty-five times about that restroom thing, and still He hadn't changed it.

"But ours are so awful," I argued aloud to Grandma, but I really only wanted to make "word noise" so I wouldn't think about the sad feelings taking me over.

"We'll go on to our church. I told you we could go to the bazaar today, anyway. Can you wait?"

"Sure," I whispered as we hurried. "Sure."

I didn't know if I could wait, though. Our church was Bethel AME on Broadway. That was a short distance from downtown. Could I make it there? And what about little Conrad? I knew he must have to go too, but he was just being quiet, holding it all in.

I was very upset with God that day as I held tight, trying not to wet my pants until we got to the church. Just as we pulled up in front of the church, I saw Christmas banners and lights.

There was a sign directing us down to the basement. How I loved that church! It had always been filled with people and suppers and music and toys and coloring books. But even more, it felt like a place where I could really talk to God. Just as we came through the door, I was praying, "Dear God, please let me make it! Please!" We ran downstairs to the sound of chatter and the tune of "Santa Claus Is Coming to Town." I rushed through a maze of tables filled with wondrous objects to reach the restroom as fast as I could.

When we went back upstairs to join the others, I looked around the room. There were brightly colored wrappings, peppermint candy, and windmills. And oh, my, what foods could smell that good? I saw fudge and chicken wings and hot biscuits. Mothers and grandmothers were floating among the tables with smiles on their faces as they touched and picked up all the fun things on display.

"Welcome, glad you all could stop by." That's what everybody said as they flashed warm smiles and showed us their preowned clothing, Christmas decorations, jewelry, and whatnots. All of the stuff had been cleaned, starched, pressed, shined, and spit polished.

"This is the Lord's shop," Grandma India said. "We can open our eyes to his abundance for us."

We stayed there for at least two hours. And for the first time in my life, I got to really shop. I felt so happy to have a place like that just for us and whispered, "Thank you, God."

Mother Lois took me aside and gave me a whole dollar. I bought mittens, a dress for my dolly, and summer sandals. Then I found a wool scarf for Grandma for just ten cents, and socks for Conrad for three pennies. The daylight was quickly running away to hide in the clouds.

As we left, each of us held full bags of wonderful things, Christmas-wrapped for beneath the tree. Grandma had Christmas garlands and a ton of gold and silver ornaments.

There were happy moments in my childhood, too. On this particular Christmas, I was overjoyed to find a place where we belonged, where we could touch the merchandise and behave as though we were free and equal.

"Praise God. Merry Christmas!" Grandma said as we got into the car.

All the way home, we sang Christmas spirituals like "Go Tell It on the Mountain" and "Silent Night."

"We are indeed blessed," Grandma said as we unloaded the car.

"Indeed." Mother Lois said, "Blessed."

I couldn't stop smiling as I laid my head on my pillow that night. I thought to myself that if we'd been able to go to the bathroom downtown, if the white people didn't own the good bathrooms, we might never have stopped by the church and gone to the party. The joy and freedom of the church Christmas doings kept my spirit up for the entire weekend. We were all joyous anticipating the cozy days together ahead of us. My happiness was so overflowing that nothing could destroy it.

# CHAPTER 14
## SANTA IS IN TOWN

**AT GIBBS ELEMENTARY SCHOOL,** the Monday morning before Christmas, all the students in grades one through six were excited with talk of the Christmas play. We sat at our desks quietly while Mrs. Backus, our teacher, dictated the spelling words we had to learn by that Friday. She said if we behaved, we could sing Christmas carols.

Since it was so cold outside, we remained inside at recess and began decorating our Christmas tree. Singing Christmas carols and getting all the words straight helped keep my attention on the joy right in front of me. I couldn't help smiling and feeling that warm spirit building inside of me. There were the glittering ornaments and the tree that Mr. Backus had brought in from his tree farm. It all made me feel very special.

By this time, I had divided my classmates into three groups. My A group were those I talked to every day. They didn't stop talking when I walked near, and they didn't make fun of my homemade clothing. Instead they greeted me with a smile and wanted to include me in all of their games and their gossip.

Group B talked to me sometimes, made cutting remarks to me when they didn't like my clothing, and often excluded me from their games, their secrets, and their gossip.

Group C often pretended I didn't exist at all. They were not always nice to me. Sometimes they made fun of me because they said I had a big chest. They called me "bra girl." I tried to hunch over to hide my growing body, but it did no good. It made me feel powerless, because there was absolutely nothing I could do about it except continue to hide. I never got an invitation from them to go to their birthday parties or their houses for playtime. They made fun of me for my high grades, my size, and my clothing.

It was hurtful when they talked about these things. We just couldn't afford the clothing from the downtown stores. Grandma would sympathize with me and make one more thing out of the flour sacks or secondhand material or even cut up her own clothing to make me something new. Whatever she did, it couldn't measure up to their store-bought clothing.

Still, it was a special day, and no matter what the other students did or said to me, they couldn't break my spirit.

During recess, Dolores, a girl from the B group, came over to join my A-group friends and me in a game of jacks. I wondered if she came over because she saw how happy I was. We were pleased to have her join us.

During these cold winter days, I grew weary of being indoors because that is when my friends seemed to tease me more. We were all mischievous because we felt cooped up and anxious. I loved being in my classroom with its plants, the big fish tank, and mahogany desks. But I liked it best when we got recess out of doors both morning and afternoon. I was always happy to return to the warm, welcoming space after I had run free.

Whenever a winter day kept us inside, there was always the chance that Mrs. Backus would ask one of us to read aloud, which made me nervous. What if I didn't know a word? That would be so embarrassing. But my teacher often told me I was doing very well, and when she promoted me to the highest book reading level in our classroom, I wanted to reach out and shake her hand.

As I said my thank-you to her, I remembered all those nights I had spent on Grandma India's lap when I was younger. She had taught me to read in order to help cure my whooping cough and asthma. At the time, I thought it was a real awful curse happening to me, but instead, it turned out to be a big blessing. Grandma said that was always the way it was in life.

. . .

Back at home we had fallen head over heels into the Christmas spirit and preparing for our yearly donation. Each year we gave away toys and clothing so that those less fortunate could enjoy Christmas as well. As with all the years before, Grandma warned us that we could not donate clothes and toys that we didn't love. We could not expect Santa to give us anything if we only put our tattered, abandoned toys in the giveaway box.

"Never mind choosing things you don't treasure," Grandma always said as we struggled to gather up the items we were giving away. "I want you to give things that are dear to you, things that bring tears to your eyes, things you'll miss."

I knew I would have to give up my long, tall rag doll, Mellie. She was just as tall as I was, and I could hardly think of life without her. But on that night as I tucked her in, I whispered to her that this would be one of the last nights we could be together. I told her we would always love each other and that Grandma was insisting I give her away because she was so precious. I knew she would make some other little girl very happy. I don't know if Mellie cried at the thought, but I surely cried into my pink satin pillow that night.

Every evening during the pre-Christmas season, we would

bake cookies and sit at the dining room table to have cookies and milk while Grandma read to us and we made gifts for each other. Sometimes she would read to us about Christmas. At other times, she would read her favorite authors.

Grandma told us we got stars in our heavenly crown if we made gifts for each other from scratch. For the last few weeks, I had sneaked into the hall closet and looked beneath her bed to search for what she called "Santa's work." She was making all kinds of sock dolls, crocheting little handkerchiefs to cover the arms of chairs and centers of tables, knitting sweaters for Conrad and me, making sweet-smelling soap, as well as whittling fun wooden toys. It made us giggle, Conrad and me, just to imagine what she might be making for us this year.

Right before Christmas, Papa Will arrived with a huge, lush green tree. He loaded it into the house and pounded it into a stand. This year, watching some of the Christmas shows on television as we decorated our tree made it seem like an even bigger party. Spending time together around that newly decorated tree with its aroma of pine filled us with jokes and hugs and laughter. Our behavior resembled that of the people on TV, happy and carefree. I was certain this would finally be the time that Papa and Mother would come back together, and we would be a family all under one roof again. I was disappointed when he bid us good night and headed for the front door.

The big family Christmas dinner was different that year.

We met at the beautiful new house of Mother's older brother, Uncle Charlie, and his wife, Aunt Annie, and their new baby, Larry. There were the usual band of close relatives, and then some new ones, because folks had gotten married. We were fifteen adults and six children.

I kept my eye on the door, watching and waiting for Papa Will to arrive. When we were eating what the grownups called hors d'oeuvres, Mother took Conrad and me aside to tell us that this year Papa Will would not be coming to join us. My spirits became all lumpy and dropped to my toes. I could feel tears burn just beneath the surface of my pretend smile as I put Papa out of my thoughts and listened to the cheerful chatter all around.

As we gathered around the table, I couldn't help admiring the special china and crystal. The plates had pears with a red shiny stem painted in the center. Conrad made the mistake of reaching for food before the blessing. He had at least ten adult relatives pointing at him all at once. Apologizing, he whispered a Bible verse, and we sat quietly listening to Grandma India say the special prayer. Then, and only then, did Uncle Charlie put the huge carving knife to the goose.

Auntie Annie's food was delicious because she was a professional chef who made up the menus and cooked for the white high schools. Her very special marinated goose, smoked turkey, and honey-glazed ham and all the trimmings made the base of a meal that everybody contributed to. I awaited Grandma India's special desserts and the gift opening that followed.

As we gathered about the tree to exchange gifts, Uncle Charlie told Christmas stories to the children and then the adults spoke of all the blessings they had enjoyed during the year. After opening our toys, we kids were ushered into the next room to play with each other.

I couldn't help thinking how much I wished Papa Will had come.

# CHAPTER 15
## TELEVISION AND BOMB SHELTERS

*AFTER THE NEW YEAR, IN 1951,* Grandma had to go back to work and Mother Lois had to go back to teach her classes, as her school started a week before ours did. Conrad and I had our way with the television.

This meant that I had so many more chances to see the news about other places and other people. One thing I noticed was lots and lots of talk about a place called Korea. We had American soldiers fighting there. The more I learned about Korea, the more I was afraid we could be bombed right at our own house in Little Rock, Arkansas. Now, in addition to worrying about the Ku Klux Klan coming to get us in the night, I started to worry every moment about being bombed.

We were also at war with Russia. It was called a Cold War, because it wasn't a fighting war, but one made up of words and deeds and threats of bad things. Every day as I watched news on the TV, read the newspaper, or listened to the radio, the newsmen were all saying we needed bomb shelters, places underground where people were going to hide when Russia came and dropped bombs on us.

But I didn't know a single soul in my community who had a bomb shelter. I decided we desperately needed to find out the location of the nearest bomb shelter so we could get there fast if we needed to. But what if white people owned it and wanted to keep us out, like they did with everything else? I clipped a plan out of a magazine for building a small one.

But Grandma warned me not to bother Mother with my silliness. "God will be our bomb shelter," she claimed.

The more I thought about it, though, the more I knew He was too busy with everybody else to concentrate on just me and my family.

The bomb shelter subject stuck in my brain. All that talk of the war we were fighting in Korea made a lot more people on television discuss bomb shelters. Why we should build them, where to build them, what size they should be. I listened to the talk and watched the TV and couldn't stop thinking about it.

Consumed by the topic, I brought it up at school, only to discover I was the only student completely informed about bomb shelters and their purpose. When I wanted to share my information about bomb shelters, most of the students stared at me as if I were from another planet. I asked all my friends at school if any of them had a bomb shelter anyway, because I wanted to reserve space in it if they did.

Each night, as I laid my head on the pillow, bomb shelters were my topic for thoughts, nightmares, dreams, and planning. I had figured out that if the white people were so unwilling to share all the things like the buses, they certainly weren't going to share their bomb shelters with us. After I talked to Grandma about it, I knew that there were no bomb shelters in our neighborhood and there wouldn't be any.

The news stories always put me right back into my pity pot, though, showing me again and again that I needed a bomb shelter. One program was about a woman in Los Angeles who was making a big to-do about building her bomb shelter. She listed all the movie stars, some of whom I absolutely worshiped, who were insisting on having bomb shelters installed in their backyards. She showed pictures and shared prices: the average cost for one was $1,995.

When I heard that, I knew we would never be able to afford to have a bomb shelter. Mother and Grandma were always counting their pennies to keep us fed as it was. Whenever Conrad and I pleaded with them for new crayons or toys from the five-and-dime, they said we needed to control our wants because God would take care of us.

Somehow, I always felt I had lots of needs He didn't seem to get around to taking care of. Not just bomb shelters, but things like new clothes that looked like the ones the kids wore on TV. Grandma and Mother Lois made some of our clothes out of old flour sacks that Grandma would soak and then turn into nice cloth. We always looked neat and clean, but it wasn't the same as the other kids who had store-bought clothes.

We didn't eat fancy meals like some of the ones I saw on TV or even at my friends' homes. There were no steaks or lamb chops. But Grandma could still stretch one chicken through an entire week of meals and keep all of us going.

Watching the television gave me a new set of worries about war and bomb shelters, but it also opened up whole new worlds. It was as though the people on television had moved in with us and extended our family. Grandma and Mother's lecturing certainly hadn't cut down on our television time. In order to watch it, we had gotten faster at doing our homework and chores. We made sure we had everything done, then we watched television. Lots and lots of television.

Despite Grandma India's grumbling, television took over our household. It gobbled up much of our family's together time while we all sat staring at the screen as though hypnotized, watching Henry Aldrich or *The Ed Sullivan Show*. I couldn't believe the kitchen gadgets, pretty furniture, shiny cars, and great toys the white families had in their homes. I saw over and over again that we weren't living equal to the people on TV. I'd sure never known any of my people who did, except maybe the church bishop and his wife.

But I was excited about something else that I saw on television. Up until that time, I had only seen our people in the pages of *Ebony* magazines. I read every word about people like Lena Horne, Harry Belafonte, and Eartha Kitt—real stars. Now, on the TV screen, they came alive. And the white people all around them seemed to welcome them and treat them as equals. They were all in such beautiful places, with beautiful things and luxuries I had never imagined. Best of all, they were right there in our living room.

Then, I noticed that while they were on TV singing or dancing or serving the white folks, none of them were in the family shows. They weren't really equal. I didn't get to see our families or their homes or furniture or anything. When I asked Grandmother India why, she said it just wasn't our turn yet.

"Have faith and keep praying," she told me.

But praying wasn't going to change the fact that I got to see whole new ways in which white folks were in charge. They had private clubs, better jobs, and better schools. Nobody tried to tell them how to choose jobs or schools, where they could live, where they could shop, or where they went to the

bathroom. They always did what was best for them. As far as I could tell, they preferred to pretend we didn't exist, except when we got in their way.

The only one of our people who I felt was in charge of his life was the singer Nat "King" Cole. I felt so happy when I watched him sing. He had such a great voice, and he seemed like such a nice man—so calm, so quiet. When he had conversations with Perry Como or other white television hosts, when he sang on their shows, they all seemed to respect him. It made me think that if he could be free and respected and accepted by all people around the world, then so could I. But I knew that unless things changed a lot—unless we had a big, big Little Rock miracle, I had to get out of that city if I ever wanted to be somebody and be free.

Watching the TV convinced me more than ever there was an incredible world beyond Little Rock where I should struggle to go. I had to be responsible for my own escape, and I could see from watching television the reality of what I wanted.

# CHAPTER 16
## FINDING MY PIECE OF THE PIE

**CONRAD AND I CONTINUED TO** sit in chairs staring at the TV screen day after day. I began to daydream that I had a pretty modern house and a pretty modern dress just like the people on the screen. More importantly, I began to see more and more black people on that screen, and I realized they seemed contented, confident, rich, and free. They had everything I thought I wanted. At first I wasn't concerned that their appearances on screen were few and far between, because I was so overjoyed that they were there at all.

I saw black people dressed beautifully, performing on television programs like *The Ed Sullivan Show*, where the host greeted them with respect and admiration. It wasn't often, but I saw my own people looking as though they were having a good life. I wanted the same freedom and the ability to make a choice about what I wanted to do when I grew up.

I went to Grandma and explained to her once again that now I knew that if we went up North, we could have all of the things that I longed for. She said I had to be quiet and patient and start writing in my diary again. She wanted me to write about my gratitude for at least one big thing that was happening and describe how it affected my life.

But she also explained to me that it was okay to want these things and to want to go North, for the truth was, if somebody baked a pie in the kitchen where a whole crowd of people with knives were about to cut into that pie, you had to get into the kitchen quickly to get your share. To get my slice of life, she said, I had to go where the pie was, get my knife out, and cut it. She admitted that in Little Rock nobody was going to give me a knife or let me anywhere near the pie of abundance.

For my people, the pie was never in the South. I knew for certain that to have my slice, I would have to get out.


Mother decided she would enroll me in music lessons to distract me and give me a new creative goal to work on. It was also my reward for making excellent grades and not talking to others about our mistreatment by the white people. I had long been intrigued by the piano, and I could hear a song

on the radio and pick the notes out on the piano keys. Even though we couldn't afford a piano, my keyboard was on paper on my dining room table.

Because I had turned nine, I could walk alone to Mrs. Hinton's house for my music lesson on Tuesday afternoons. I counted it as time when I could daydream or worry about anything I wanted. I actually scheduled times for worrying. During the two-block walk back and forth, I could think about things and try to figure them out.

My worries about having a bomb shelter and about the war in Korea began to grow again because there was so much talk about General MacArthur on the television news. I supposed he had done something wrong, because President Truman took away his job. I was also worried because as they said in the papers, they were taking away the man who had been there the longest and probably knew the most about keeping the Koreans from sending a bomb on us.

One day I was overflowing with all these worries, hoping our neighbor, Mrs. Williams, would build a bomb shelter because they had lots more money than we did. If they built one, maybe we could chip in a few dollars and they would let us stay there. I let some of my thoughts slip out during my music lesson. My music teacher, Mrs. Hinton, told me that our folks had a lot more important things to worry about than a bomb shelter.

"We have the Klan and the white man always on our backs," she said. "They're much closer to us than the Korean War is. Let the grownups worry about those things. You should be thinking about your piano and your voice."

Then she told me, "Music quiets fears."

Taking Mrs. Hinton's advice, I began listening to more music. I even began to think that maybe I could become a singer. I watched more singing on television and added being a singing star to my daydream collection. With the right music on the radio, I could just see myself singing in front of a huge audience. I would look up places on my globe and decide if I wanted to perform there or not. I practiced "That Lucky Old Sun," a hit song on the radio sung by Frankie Laine. I heard that song all the time. The radio announcer said it was a number one top hit. I could see that Mother's plan was working because I started to get excited when I heard the songs that were on Hit Parade and the singers that sang them. There were tons of my people singing on the radio who got their songs high on *Your Hit Parade.* There were fewer on the television, but I saw that it was achievable. It gave me a real positive role model to follow. I decided this was what I was going to do: I would get my slice of the pie by becoming a singer. I was encouraged because everyone always told me I had a voice like Dinah Washington and perfect pitch.

With time devoted to television, we had to give up listening to some of our favorite radio shows like *Fibber McGee and Molly* or *Edgar Bergen and Charlie McCarthy*. Jack Benny moved to television, so we were still able to enjoy him. But weekdays, Monday through Friday, we continued having family dinners when we took time with each other. Every evening, Grandma insisted we read books around the table after dinner. That was when Mother Lois or Grandma went over our new words. We had to add one word to our vocabulary each day.

"Vocabulary is the key to success. How one speaks and presents one's grasp of the English language is vitally important," Mother said over and over again. I didn't always understand her big words, but slowly, one by one, she was teaching them to Conrad and me.

Each night we could choose a new word. She would have us write it down on slips of paper and then carry it with us until the next night when we recited its meaning to her. If we didn't yet understand the meaning of the word, we would carry it over until the next day. During the last week of February, Mama's birthday month, I chose a word I had heard on television, *apartheid*. It meant forcing black people and white people to live apart and unequal.

"It's how our people live in Africa," Mother said.

*It is also the life I live here*, I thought. I couldn't forget that word for a long, long time.

· · ·

153

My school days at Gibbs Elementary School passed quickly. My favorite classes were still math and reading because they were so easy for me. I had loved history until that spring when we began the study of slavery. Reading about it day after day made me sad. Grandma was right: We had come a long, long way. But I wanted to go a lot further. I wanted to be free—as free as any white person.

I began to get more books out of the library where my mother worked. The more I read, the angrier I became. My people had been brought here against their will—without the advantages of speaking English, understanding what democracy meant, or knowing anything about how people lived here. The incredible burden of the trip across the ocean packed into boats like sardines in a can, body to body, unable to talk to each other because they came from different and sometimes opposing tribes, was awful in itself. But to find yourself in a strange land and learn that you have become someone's chattel, property to a white stranger, was unbearable. Yet somehow, some of them survived while many others died.

I learned that the majority of the slaves worked in the cotton fields from six in the morning until nine or ten at night with only a fifteen-minute break for a meal and water. The cotton the slaves were growing became the major export for this new country. This country's economy was built and grew on the backs of slaves. Therefore, they were measured and judged by the amount of cotton they produced. When they didn't produce what the master expected, they were beaten, and some were even killed.

I started researching about our leaders, the work of the NAACP, and what they were doing to fight for our equality. I was glad to see that someone was fighting back. Mother still told me to stop my pushing, as I would get killed if I kept doing it. But these people were doing it legally—and doing it for all of us. I was so excited to discover their organized system of lawyers fighting for our equality.

I began to understand what Grandma had said about how we had come a long way. I had never understood before. Grandma said, "There is no crying, no whining, no complaining. There is just march forward, girl. You have to make sure that you are contributing to our journey forward, not sitting on the side of the road whimpering."

Slowly in my mind, I began to envision that we *could* march forward. There was a possibility for change because I saw change on the pages of the history books that I was reading.

The real questions were: How was I going to contribute to that progress, and wasn't there a way to speed it up? I wanted it to come in my lifetime.

# CHAPTER 17
## ANGEL IN A WHITE SHEET

*IN 1952, AT THE END* of the school year, Gillam Park—a park set aside just for black people—opened. There was a pool there, which I found very exciting. Many of the people in my community were unhappy, though, because it was far away in an isolated, undeveloped area, and there were no lifeguards, no shade, no phone, and only crude concrete squares for dressing rooms. Above all else, there were no concessions, merry-go-rounds, or the other amenities offered at the whites-only Fair Park, which had been promised to us. Gillam Park had nothing civilized around it and was far from a grocery store or doctor's office. If someone got into trouble or was going to drown, no timely help would be available out there.

One Saturday, there was excitement in the air because we were having a citywide, interfaith youth picnic at Gillam Park to celebrate the end of the school year. Young people from all our churches would be there. The announcement promised games and competitions. As there were no buses to carry us out there, parents had to arrange carpooling for us. My Auntie Mae agreed to drive me and some of my other Sunday school classmates and some of the kids from her church to the park in her old, wood-sided station wagon. Mother was to bring me home.

Despite the invitation, when we arrived and were dropped off, we found it wasn't at all organized. Kids sat on the ground or on large rocks in the sun. Al-

though we had been advised to bring our sun hats, not many of us had remembered. I certainly hadn't. Some kids wandered away toward the woods, looking for shade. There were no tables, chairs, or umbrellas to shade us by the pool. For as far as I could see, there was only dust, huge boulders, and thick woods. When a new car drove up, a cloud of dust blew around and into our mouths.

I'd dreamed for years of finally having a park where we could ride on the merry-go-round and eat cotton candy. I danced for joy, hopeful Gillam Park would be that place.

Everything was getting hot. There was no ice to cool our drinks or our foreheads. There was no phone around, so I could not call and tell Mother I wanted to go home early. I was too hot and queasy with a headache. With no phone, she could not call me and tell me she was going to be late.

None of the games that had been planned or competitions they wanted to have worked out because it was much too hot. I wandered around looking for an escape, as there were some cars arriving to pick people up. Other parents who had stayed at the park were leaving, too. I looked around for someone I could ask to take me home, since Mother was still not there and I had no way to contact her.

This is what I dreamed Gilllam Park would be; however, my dream was buried in granite dust and hard crusty rocks with no shade, no greenery, and no picnic tables.

In the search for shade and comfort, I had gotten separated from my friends and decided that rather than continue to search for the others I would look for the road home and make it by myself. My solo journey would prove to Mother that I was capable of going more places by myself, I thought.

Maybe I'd meet someone along the road, possibly even Mother, who would take me home. I suppose it was part of my overwhelming urge to have more freedom, to convince Mother to have more faith in me and permit me to go more places and do more things. But there I was on this rocky road with no cars and no houses, and only bushes and trees on either side of me. Never mind that my heart was up in my throat pounding like runaway drums and my stomach was squeezing and screaming pain. I refused to allow myself to be frightened.

The sun shifted overhead, and there was more shade as I walked along. I watched my shadow move. There were still no cars. The only sounds I heard were those made by small birds or animals in the brush. Several times I thought, *This is wrong—this is a big mistake, and maybe I should go back.* But when I looked back along the dirty, rocky road with the heat rising up off it, I decided I must be closer to town and should just keep going. Surely Mother was somewhere along this road.

Dusk was falling, and ahead of me was another barren, dusty road going off to the right. I had no idea where I was or which direction would lead me back home. It had been a hot day, but it was finally beginning to cool off. I was walking too fast to cool down, though—in fact I was dripping with perspiration. I was also thinking about God. Was He willing to come along with me even when I had made a conscious decision not to obey what I knew were the rules?

"Never walk alone in isolated places," Mother always said. "Stay where crowds of our folks are, especially on Friday or Saturday evenings when the Klan searches for our folks."

Again, and again, she and Grandma had repeated those warnings. I had vowed over and over that I would never, ever break those rules.

The sound of my own raspy breathing invaded my thoughts. I pleaded with God not to let all the wild green bushes and grass surrounding me bring up my asthma and allergies. What if I had an asthma attack right here—then what? I had to ignore that threat. I paused to think of what Grandma would say. She would say, *Erase all negative thoughts— listen for God's instructions. Silence and prayer, that is your need now, Melba.*

If only I could see a sign that told me what street I was on or what direction I should head in to reach home and the safety of Grandma's arms.

Just then, I heard the engine of some sort of truck coming my way. *Hide, hide in the bushes,* is what the voice in my head said. *Now! Now run!* But another voice in my head told me that if I hid, I risked being on this endless barren road after dark.

So I stood still at the side of the road. As soon as the truck turned the corner in the road, I immediately knew I'd done the wrong thing. I wanted to run and hide, but something made me stand absolutely still, while my heart pounded so hard that I was certain it would jump out of my chest.

"Get in here. We're gonna give you a ride, gal," said a rough, unkind voice.

I knew that I could not take rides with strangers, and especially not with a white stranger in a big flatbed truck with fencing around the back of it. It looked like one of those trucks that they packed Mexican workers into to haul them to pick cotton against their wills. Or at least that's what it looked like to me.

"No, sir, thank you. If you'll just point me in the direction of Cro—uh, Twelfth Street . . ." Right away I knew I shouldn't ask for directions to the real street address where I lived. "I'll be on my way." I turned right as if to make a move, and suddenly I felt an awful burn on my upper right arm before I turned to see him holding a smoking long gun.

"You ain't gonna hold us up," the man said. "Join our party, girl. Get the hell into the back of the truck and keep your proper mouth shut. Who taught you to speak in that uppity tone with those sharp words?"

I didn't know exactly what he meant, so I shut my mouth and moved toward the back of the truck, where a black hand opened the gate and reached down to me. That's when I saw that there were roughly hewn benches along each side and lots more people in there that I couldn't see when I was standing on the road. Slowly, I looked around to size up the others as I took a seat, easing down by a woman who resembled Mother Lois in her coloring.

There were two white men and eight of my people whose facial expressions told me I had a lot to worry about. The big question was where were they going and what were they going to do. Whatever it was, I was going to be a part of it against my will.

I remembered what Grandmother had often said to me: "If you know you are falling off a mountain, look around you to see what you can do to save yourself. If you see nothing available to save yourself, settle down and find peace as you wait for God to rescue you."

I tried to find peace.

There was a part of me that wanted to cry out loud for help or jump off the truck. I wanted to ask all the others where they came from and what they thought was going to happen to us. Meanwhile, I was getting more and more upset because the Klansmen were driving me back to where I had come from—back to the nowhere, dusty, rock-filled site where city officials had built the pool and recreation park for our folks.

Just then, the truck turned left into a narrower place covered with bushes. If possible, it was even more isolated than

where I had been walking. The truck drove for some time and then we entered yet another clearing where there were more trucks and more people. It had to be a huge meeting or a celebration; there were a lot of people there, and they were all wearing the Klan's sheets and masks. It was as if they were having a party, because there was food and beer on tables. I began to panic. I had to get out of there. Nothing good could be planned by these people so deep in the woods.

And what were me and my people doing in the truck? They did not have parties for or with us, so why had they brought us there?

"Let's move it. Y'all get out and get over there and don't move."

I climbed down, and we moved to the spot the man directed us to go, silent and stiff in our movements, each of us anticipating something awful. Meanwhile the Klansmen—at least fifty of them—huddled in groups, drinking their liquor in one form or another. They pointed at us and laughed out loud. I thought for a moment that some of the people in sheets might be women, but I couldn't tell for certain. I searched for a way to sneak out of that place.

Every now and then, I saw one of our women get dragged toward another clearing. I would hear them whimper and make weird noises and then go silent. Once I heard what I thought was a gunshot.

The Klansmen would come back from the bush, sometimes alone, sometimes in twos or threes, brushing themselves off. I wondered whether the girl they had taken with them got to go home. I wanted to go home, too. But I worried about what she had to do in order to go home. I hoped she would send somebody back to get us, but who would have the real courage to come? Who among our men would come into that Klan crowd to rescue us?

For some time, I had needed to go to the bathroom. I was feeling that need more intensely, but what could I do about it? The very last thing I wanted to do was to draw attention to myself. And yet I felt an urgent need. I moved closer to the man nearest to me.

"Where the hell do you think you're going?" the man who appeared to be the leader asked.

"Sir, I need to go to the bathroom."

"Where the hell did you get this sharp-talking nigger?" another Klansman asked.

"Never mind," the leader said. "I've already claimed her as my dessert. I picked her up on the side of the road. Hey, Emma, take her out there and help her stay clean until I can get to her."

The most petite sheet-wearing person touched my arm and gestured for me to walk away from that gathering toward another patch of bushes. We walked for quite a piece until she spoke to me.

"Go over there and hurry please."

"Yes, ma'am, thank you," I said. "Uh, could I ask you a question please?"

"We haven't got much time. Better hurry and go."

"Yes, ma'am. I just would like to know when they'll let me go home." I couldn't help weeping. "I wanna go home now. I've been gone all day."

"You're just a child, aren't you?" she asked. "How old are you?"

"Eleven," I told her. "Mother's looking for me by now. Please tell them it's time for me to go home."

"Good Lord, despite those large breasts, and what are you, five foot six inches? You really don't know what's going on, do you?"

"No, ma'am, I wanna go home."

"Emma, what's going on?" the leader's voice yelled at us through the darkness.

"Just taking a moment to make certain she's clean and ready for you," the woman called back. "Patience."

Then she turned back to me. "Child, I don't know where you live, but I want you to walk that way over there, where I think there are some of your folks," she said. "Now, take this rock and hit me hard here on the jaw. I'm gonna lie down right over here. Okay, hit me."

"But no, ma'am, I can't do that," I told her. "I don't hit adults."

"Do you wanna get out of here alive with your modesty

intact? Well, do you?" she asked. "Then hit me and take off. Get going, and you better take off that light-colored dress and fold it in your arms. Your black body won't be seen at night." She watched as I followed her instructions.

"Run, child, run for your life. But if you get caught, you'll need to admit you hit me."

"Yes, ma'am. I promise. Thank you, thank you for letting me go home." I didn't understand what was going on or why she wanted me to hit her or how I would get away, but I could hear Grandma saying, *March forward, girl. You got no choice but to move forward, now. Right now. God is moving you with His energy.*

I ran as fast as I could, despite my pounding heart and despite the deep cramps in my legs and my stomach. During the first few minutes, I could hear those men behind me shouting about what they would do when they got their hands on me.

I couldn't listen. I could only afford to hear God's promise to always be with me and protect me.

I don't know how long I ran, pushing my way through thick vines and bushes that tore the dress I held and scratched my legs and feet and arms until I could feel the sting and blood drawn by thorns and twigs. I fell so many times that I stopped counting. I just pulled myself up, drew deep wheezing breaths, whispered, "Thank you, God," and continued running faster than I ever knew I could.

I had no idea which way I was running, but I knew I had to continue until I saw a house that was safe. I couldn't stop where there was a fancy-looking house, an ordinary family, because it might be a Klan home. I had to find a subtler place where my folks might be. My left side hurt, and pain bit at the backs of my legs, but I had to keep going.

I don't know what time it was when I found a modest wooden home—a small place that was plain without extras. I lingered at the edge of the clearing, hoping someone might come to the front porch, but that didn't happen. I heard dogs barking in the distance. I couldn't greet any stranger carrying a dress in my hands. Although it was soaking with perspiration and blood, I put it on and walked slowly toward the front door. I was mindful that these might not be my people and that I might need to get away again. I was exhausted. I was uncertain that I could walk another step farther, let alone run.

I took a deep breath and whispered, "Please, God, please." I saw the horror of how I must look in the eyes and expression of the man who opened the door. It was a man of my color whom I did not recognize, but I fell into his arms crying, "Please, please help me."

"Hattie, Hattie, come quickly, we got us an injured gal here."

The man and woman, who looked to be the age of my grandparents, welcomed me and allowed me to take a bath. After I told them my story, they decided it would be unsafe to make a trip to my house that evening. They didn't have a phone, so I would have to wait a bit longer to see Mother and Papa Will and Grandma and Conrad.

As I climbed into bed, they told me if someone from the Klan knocked on the door, I should not come out. And if they got rowdy or violent, they said to run out of the back door and keep going. They thought the Klan would continue to search for me for a while.

After they left the room, I climbed back out of bed and got on my knees and prayed. "Thank you, God. I will not disobey again. I promise." Then I climbed back into bed. Although frightened someone might still be hunting me, I fell fast asleep in deep peace, thanking God again.

The next day Miss Hattie decided she had to disguise me as a working man—wearing coveralls, a denim jacket, and hair tucked up in an old, floppy hat. Then she reached in the fireplace for some ashes and went into the backyard for some dirt. She stirred it together, then smeared it on my face and hands. That way, I wouldn't be easily recognized as we made our way to my house.

I was nervous as we rode to my house, but so grateful to think I'd be safe and see my family again. When we arrived, many family members were gathered in mourning with a minister leading prayer. At first, they didn't recognize me in my workingman clothes.

Then I called out, "Grandma, Grandma, I'm home."

"Praise God! You come here to me," she said.

That's when I burst into tears. I didn't think I would ever feel her arms around me again. I wondered what they would say to me and how they would chastise me for frightening them that way. To my amazement, they said only words of welcome to me and words of gratitude to Mr. Packer, the man who had brought me home.

"Thank goodness there is no school today," Mother said, after Mr. Packer left, loaded down with Grandma's fresh-baked cookies and a roasted chicken that was to be our dinner.

They did not ask what happened to me but instead asked me to join them in thanking God once more before they sent me to take a long, long nap.

After a lunch of rice and beans, they pulled me into the dining room and shut the door tight. As I tearfully unraveled my story of the truck and the Klansmen, they were obviously unnerved and tearful.

Mother said, "We are all so blessed, child. You could so easily have gone home to the Lord. God is good to us. We will pray for blessings on that woman who saved your life, and in the meantime, you will understand that not all white people have chosen to behave the same. We will wait for your father to come, and we will talk about how to disguise you, because you can't look the same—the Klan will still be looking for you. You are on lockdown until at least the end of the year. You can't go anywhere without an adult. We will take you to school and pick you up."

# CHAPTER 18
## WHO IS JIM CROW?

**PAPA ARRIVED BACK ABOUT THREE P.M.** and took a seat in the dining room with us. I could see by his damp eyes, set chin, and steely expression that I was in trouble. Looking at me with a stern stare he said, "I see, child, that you've had a major lesson in disobeying your parents. Why did you decide that was a good idea? You frightened us to death. We sat up all night praying for you."

"No, sir, no, sir, I'll never, ever do it again." I looked down at the floor; I did not look directly into his eyes.

Grandma interrupted. "What would it have been like had you never come home? I can't even explain to you. No words can tell you how we felt."

"I don't know what you were thinking," Mother said, "at that time of the evening, to take off by yourself."

I was so frightened to hear them talking to me that way and to see their drawn and sad faces, and I knew things would be different from now on.

Papa said, "It's really clear that we must disguise this girl to keep her safe. It's absolutely necessary."

At this point, Grandma said, "I think we should give some consideration to the Asian art of binding the chest. That would rid her of one distinct physical characteristic and alter her appearance considerably."

Mother responded, "Yes, and we should brush her hair back off her face—pull it back and tuck it under and tie it down, so as to take the attention off her long wavy locks."

Papa added, "I'll get her some fake horn-rimmed glasses to wear."

At that moment, I wanted to disagree, because it all sounded too severe. I wanted to object, but I just asked a question: "Isn't that too much?" I would never get a boy to look at me if they did that. Tears began to seep into my eyes as I thought how I would look to all my friends.

Tears were brimming in Papa's eyes, too, and he said, "Look here, girl, the goal is to keep you with us forever."

That began my emergence as a new and dreary person. It made me more quiet and more submissive. I stopped my social crusade to fit in among the popular students in my

class. Something had happened to me during that encounter with the Klan. I knew something even more awful could have happened to me. I also began to understand that the separate water fountains and schools, were based on something. It was a system. It was a ratified, agreed-upon system.

I wondered what might be the reason. I talked to my mother and grandmother, and they began to tell me about Jim Crow. The words were familiar to me, because I had heard the phrase in class, though I had paid them little attention at the time. I wanted to learn who Jim Crow was, though.

Mother told me, "To be a true student, you can read what is happening now, but you need to do research into the past to find out more, because history always repeats itself."

I wanted to find out where the permission came from that allowed them to treat us as badly as they did now. My grandmother told me to look up the Plessy decision. She even offered to drive me to the library.

"It's time you understand exactly what is going on so you can help us save your life," Mother said, as she opened the door to get out of the car.

Plessy turned out to be a heart-wrenching case about an African-American man named Homer Adolph Plessy who wanted to take a ride on the train in 1892. He decided to take a seat in a car marked WHITES ONLY. At that time, the law said that blacks could not sit in the same car as whites. So repeatedly, the white folks asked him to get up, but he refused to leave. Homer Plessy was arrested and convicted of violating the Separate Car Act in Louisiana. But Mr. Plessy fought back, hoping to show that the law was unfair. In 1896, the Supreme Court heard his case, but they ruled eight to one that the separate-but-equal doctrine was not in violation of his constitutional rights.

The court somehow found that the separate-but-equal law was not in violation of the Thirteenth Amendment to the Constitution, which abolished slavery, or the Fourteenth Amendment, which enforced the absolute equality between the races before the law. Justice Henry Brown explained that separate but equal was just fine. White people felt equal, after all, so why should black people feel any different?

Ultimately in the Plessy v. Ferguson hearing, the court ruled in favor of the Jim Crow laws. When I read that, I thought to myself, *What are the Jim Crow laws?* I went to the library at the Baptist College and asked the librarian about the Jim Crow laws. She directed me to a book, which I checked out.

The book said that the Jim Crow laws, which had been in effect since the 1880s, divided whites and blacks into two separate worlds. I was astonished to find there were real laws set up to justify mistreating us. Those laws said whites and blacks should be separated in all public places: drinking fountains, parks, trains, buses, downtown food counters, and public schools. These laws went unchallenged for many years. During that time, African-Americans throughout the whole county were treated as second-class citizens.

One of the ways the laws were enforced was by lynching. Lynching was defined as execution by being hanged from a rope. My mind went immediately to Mr. Harvey, the man who had been lynched in my great-grandmother's church. The Klan still killed our people that way, without fear of being arrested or tried. I read that between the years 1880 and 1930, over 3,744 black men and women and children, mostly Southerners, were said to have been lynched in the United States. Suddenly I was overcome with grief. All those innocent men, women, and children died like Mr. Harvey in great pain. Why?

Discovering that there were real laws and not just unwritten traditions that doomed us to that way of life made me even more depressed and frightened because now I knew white people had been given the absolute legal right to treat us as second-class citizens.

# CHAPTER 19
## MY LIFE FORGES AHEAD

**BY AGE TWELVE, I WAS** officially an eighth-grader and was madly in love with my life as a student at Dunbar Junior and Senior High. What I liked most was moving from class to class. I felt awake and alive. I liked picking up my book satchel each time the bell rang and looked forward to talking about something entirely different the next period. I was excited every day now.

Mother sometimes would buy me a new skirt or would sew a blouse for me out of store-bought material. I got a real quilted skirt and crinoline slip. I felt like somebody important. But more than anything, I was so happy in junior high because I didn't stand out anymore. Many of the students were also getting taller, and I had a friend who was my exact height. I felt so much more comfortable standing and talking with her in the hallway and walking home with her.

Another good thing about junior high was my home economics class. One of my neighbors, Mrs. Carmella Jobson, taught the course, and I loved going into her class to cook and bake things. That whole class allowed for time to joke and be happy with other students. During all of my other classes, we were told not to talk to each other, but in home ec, we could talk as we learned the art of fine cooking. It was a course every girl took who expected to be a lady, according to Grandma. There wasn't a boy in sight during that period, so we talked a lot about them.

For once in my life, I went with my friends to Woolworth. I took this photo, and for just a moment pretended I was free and equal and happy.

In the newspaper, I read about a new person, Dwight Eisenhower, who had become president in January of 1953. When he first took over, I had wondered if things would really begin to change across America and in Little Rock. There was a possibility, I thought, because Grandma told me that former President Truman had put African-American and white soldiers together in the armed forces during his term. Before that, African-American soldiers had separate sleeping places, separate units, and separate everything. Now African-American and white soldiers shared things like sleeping quarters, meals, equipment, foxholes, trains, planes, and cars. They also had some of the same opportunities for promotion.

But after President Eisenhower had been in office almost a year, nothing was different. I decided that I would stop hoping some white man would be kind and make changes from afar. I had in mind that I could make positive change, but every time I made a suggestion to Grandma or Mother, they said they did not have the money or an attorney to back me up, and I would get killed if I showed any public sign of not obeying the white people. Therefore, the only hope I had was faith in God and my letters to Him. I had to trust God to someday take charge and change everything.

Those days I wanted more than ever to be able to go to a movie theater and to see a 3D movie. The newspapers and magazines kept showing pictures of audiences staring at movie screens through dark glasses with white paper frames. I was so jealous. My letter to God was extra long and extra angry the night I first saw pictures of those audiences.

When I read that maybe we would get to sit in the balcony of some white movie houses, I felt a little spark of hope. Up until then, the only place I could go to the movies was in the old, ratty, smelly Gem Theatre on Ninth Street, in what Grandma India called our "sin district" of town. It was lined with pool halls and honky-tonk nightclubs and liquor stores. Going to the Gem meant walking past staggering loudmouth drunks and being around seedy-looking people who frightened us. We seldom, if ever, were willing to take that risk, so we didn't get to see movies. I pined in my heart to be in a dark theater with popcorn and larger-than-life actors on the screen in the latest hit movie.

But I had yet another new problem to worry about. The boys began to tease me more harshly and more frequently about my growing breasts, making me want to hide. These boys didn't use polite terms like "breasts," but instead they said terrible things. The worst part was that they talked very loudly. I was so upset one day that I let go and ran to the bathroom. I tried not to cry aloud. I was still teary-eyed when I arrived home to have craft time with Grandma India. She said I was just growing up, and that I should have pride in myself.

Then the next Saturday, Grandma and Mother took me to town. They made Conrad stay with Dad because they said it was a girl's special day. They took me to the department store and announced they were going to buy me a bra.

The bra fit fine, but now my chest rose to mounds and was pointed. *You'd have to be blind not to see them,* I thought as I looked into the mirror, surveying my profile in my favorite pink organdy dress with a fitted waist and a sash tied in the back.

Sure enough, back at school, whenever I went outside at recess to play volleyball or any game where people came close to me, somebody always pointed to my bra because the straps showed. Long ago I had been forced to give up climbing on the monkey bars and the swings as well, which had made me very sad. Now I would have to give up volleyball and track. I was so jealous of the smaller girls who didn't need bras. Their bodies were the right size for a twelve-year-old.


One day in early April, during recess, Mrs. Butler ushered us outside on the playground and measured us for the Maypole dance. "No," she said to me, loud enough for the world to hear. "Melba Joy Pattillo, you've got uh—your boobs speak to the audience. They call attention to you and you only. You'll look so much older than the others that the audience will think you were kept back," she stuttered, staring at my breasts. "I'm sorry but you absolutely cannot be in the Maypole dance."

After school, I walked as fast as I could, lickety-split, up the street and across the persimmon field. I cried all the way home. I could not believe that now another thing was making me unwelcome, not just in the white world because of my color, but even in my own school because my body was growing faster than that of the other girls.

By the time I had celebrated my twelfth birthday back on December 7, 1953, I'd believed I had put aside my hurt over being left out of all the Maypole dances forever. My feelings weren't hurt as much when I wasn't included in other programs and dance lessons with the boys, either. However, when she said this again, I was hurt and all my former attempts to adjust to peacefully watching from the sidelines and not having to sweat all that rehearsing and stage fright were in vain.

Two things that comforted me and quieted my worries, making everything wonderful, were being in church on Sunday and sitting all alone in my room listening to music. I loved it when we arose early and got to church as other people were arriving. That meant I could get a Sunday school seat by the handsome boy I liked to stare at. We girls giggled and tossed pennies back and forth into our teacher Miss Stiles's chair before she arrived. She would gather the pennies and put them in the collection plate. She always reviewed our obligations to God and why we had a debt to pay to our brothers and sisters. Our obligation was to see all people as humans and to do unto others as we would have them do unto us. Then she would explain that meant everybody, white people included.

I loved Bethel AME church, always filled with friendly smiling faces, as well as Reverend Young and his family. The big old stone building was three stories high and had been a part of my life since I was a baby. It was almost a magical place, where only good things happened to me and everybody there showered me with smiles.

At least three times a week, I looked forward to Mother Lois taking me to Bethel AME for choir practice, speeches by people from out of town who talked about God, and Bible study. The choir was led by a friend of

At fourteen, I attended my first church dance and received my first corsage from a boy. Mother chaperoned the dance and was looking on from a place in the corner.

Mother's who had a beautiful voice. I imagined her as a lovely colorful bird that could fly if she chose when she played the piano, and her voice soared in the most hypnotic tones. No matter what I was doing, I always stopped when she stood in front of the choir and either raised her hands to direct them or stood at the piano and started to sing. How I wished she led the Junior Choir, which I was in.

When I began to think about what it meant to feel safe, I had to admit that church was the only place outside my home where once again I felt perfectly, absolutely, secure. It's not that I didn't remember Mr. Harvey's death and think about him, especially because suddenly a big row was being made over the hanging of my people. The newspapers carried stories about objections to black people being hanged. Only the state had permission to hang anyone, people argued, and that was after a trial. Now, for the first time, lynchings were being publicly spoken about in the news, whereas before they seemed to be a silent hobby of the white folks.

This didn't stop the Klan from continuing to ride on weekends and white people from treating us as though they hated us. They still hanged black people as a form of punishment for the smallest of deeds, but at Bethel AME, every member of the church was welcome and loved.


By this time, I had begun to realize that I truly loved music. My teachers said I had an "ear." I could tell the difference between popular tunes and the blues. I liked them both, and I could easily identify the notes so that I could play them on a piano.

I loved watching *The Perry Como Show,* and I found myself totally enchanted by Nat "King" Cole and the song "Too Young." I sang it again and again, and every time Grandma would allow me to crank her Victrola, that's what I would play.

Mrs. Hinton said my piano and voice were coming along just fine. In time, I became fearless about standing up and singing a song on stage. When I sang a song on stage by my-self, I was totally in charge.

I was spending considerable time out of school, especially during the months of December, January, and February, because of my asthma. During that time, Grandma and the television became my tutor. I would learn information and familiarize myself with ways to categorize it along certain topic lines. I held many debates with Mother, Grandma, and other adults. I was also learning to breathe despite my asthma so I could keep on singing.

Grandma urged me to read more books and the right magazines: *Life, Look,* and news magazines like *Time.* She would find things that I might be interested in and have me read them. Usually it would be about show business or stars in the movies or television. She avoided articles that might make me worry.

I also started reading about sports figures in the newspapers, specifically about Jackie Robinson. His championship playing didn't just get him into the major league; it got him the Most Valuable Player award in 1949 and had proved him to be an All-Star player for the last five years.

That summer, the newspaper said that he and his team were on the way to another World Series. As we looked at his photo, tears crept into Grandma's eyes. "Well, I don't want to hear you complain about answers to your prayers. That Mr. Jackie Robinson playing again in that big game is an answer. You just don't realize it yet."

"Oh, yes, Grandma, I do realize it. Mr. Robinson went where he was not welcome and has made space for himself and our folk who will live even a hundred years from now. We all have to praise him."

Grandma smiled. "Exactly. It is as though he is clearing a trail for us to follow, and of course we are making steps forward here that we must be grateful for."

"You mean like the pool and the movies," I said.

On the same day of my thirteenth birthday dinner, Conrad got his thirteenth Boy Scout badge, so we had a double celebration. Mother Lois had bought me a piano for my birthday. I thought I would burst with excitement when the knock came and two men rolled a piano in through the front door. I wasn't going to tear up the paper keyboard I had been practicing on for the last three years, though. I carefully folded it and placed it in the drawer with my Bible.

Grandma had a smug grin on her face and agreed to allow me to stop my afternoon reading that day so I could sit down and touch the keys, dust the cover, and try to play the songs in the new book of show tunes that came with it. It was a mahogany spinet, and it was shiny and beautiful. Grandmother said it was not secondhand but brand-new, right from the factory. I couldn't believe my eyes.

I could hardly get through my official birthday dinner that Sunday afternoon and our usual Sunday ride. Mother Lois took us for a ride along University Avenue near the University of Arkansas school building where she had attended classes.

Next, she drove all the eight blocks around Central High School. It stretched from Fourteenth to Sixteenth on Park Street, and was two blocks across. There were green playing fields and such and a huge sand-colored brick building that looked almost like a castle.

Central High's building was so tall and so stately that I thought it looked like a university as well. It seemed like there were acres and acres of grass and a pond and wonderful shrubs. It might have been the tallest building in Little Rock. I wondered what was inside. There must be a lot of things on those seven floors.

After the ride, we went for double-decker ice cream cones, which was my family's choice for a special treat. It seemed to me that life was slowly getting better. I was hearing about progress being made across the country for my people. It felt to me as though my world was getting bigger, and I was getting familiar with this big world, meeting more people and doing more things. I felt a quiet sense of peace.

# CHAPTER 20
## MARCHING FORWARD

**MAY 17, 1954, WAS THE DAY** when God gave me a huge answer to my prayers about being equal, even though it didn't feel like an answer at first—and I didn't understand how huge the blessing was, nor how it would change my life. I knew it was a huge jolt forward in my time.

My teacher, Miss Carpenter, announced that the Supreme Court had ruled that separate was not equal. I could have told them that, if they'd asked me, of course, but now it was official. In a legal case called Brown v. Board of Education of Topeka, Kansas, the Court had said that separate public schools for whites and African-Americans were not equal.

The court case was about Linda Brown, an eight-year-old African-American girl from Topeka, Kansas, who lived

Seeing Mother in the library studying so intensely inspired me to want to do the same thing.

four blocks from an elementary school, but because she was African-American, she was unable to enroll there. Instead, she had to travel twenty-five blocks away by bus to another school that was set up for our people. Her father, Oliver Brown, applied to the school board to have her transferred to the closer school. When he was turned down, he sued the board of education. This case was taken up by the NAACP and brought to the Supreme Court two years later. A highly respected African-American attorney named Thurgood Marshall worked on the case for the NAACP. The Supreme Court decided that as far as schools and education were concerned, the separate-but-equal concept did not apply, because the facilities provided were always unequal.

I was breathless. I couldn't believe what was happening. Of course, I ached to get hold of a newspaper so I could learn more. I wanted to rush home to talk with Grandma.

When I arrived home, the talk about the Brown decision was making everyone watch the news. Grandma and Mother were discussing what they thought the decision would mean for our future. More opportunities? There had been whispers of some of Little Rock schools being integrated. Some of our students had tried to enter Little Rock's Central High School before but had been turned back. Television and radio were flooded with the news.

When I talked to Grandma, she said, "These are possibilities. Slow down! Wait on the Lord. Don't get ahead of yourself. Be grateful."

I was compelled to read the newspaper longer and to look up more words in the dictionary every day. I had to learn as much as I could about the court ruling that was exciting to our entire community and upsetting them at the same time. People were really frightened of what the white community would do to them, because the ruling was making white people extremely angry. That Supreme Court ruling, which said separate schools for our people and whites were not equal, was causing an uproar because now all the white officials were writing in the newspaper and speaking on radio and television, saying that they would never allow us to go to their schools no matter what, even though this decision was supposed to compel them to do so.

I wondered if the Supreme Court knew what they were doing when they made that announcement. There were so many things to worry about that I couldn't even count them all. First of all, loud and angry crowds of white people had now begun to gather in rallies in public places, shouting that we would never sit in their schools beside their children. While I was frightened of the rallies, I was also hopeful that the Supreme Court order would mean not only that I would be going to their schools, but soon be sitting at the lunch counters and going to movies that were currently reserved for whites only.

Five days later, the Little Rock School Board published their statement saying that the district had been working on a plan to provide separate but equal opportunities for all the children in the city. "The response of all our citizens has made it possible to have and maintain our schools in their present form. Despite the Supreme Court decision, we will maintain our present program," they wrote in the newspaper.

Right away Grandma said that meant they were not going to do anything different. A few days later, to our joy, Virgil Blossom, the superintendent of schools, announced that while they had this present program, they also agreed that somehow, they had to abide by the laws of the land. The white school board knew that the rest of the white community was set against integration. They also knew that the black community had been longing for the opportunity to break down barriers that had been in place for years and achieve a better education for their children.

By reading the paper, we discovered that once again they were in charge and would work to prevent our getting the full benefit of our rights. Their plan was designed to keep integration at a minimum. They were building Horace Mann High School for one thousand black students to be opened in 1956 and Hall High School for one thousand white students to be opened in 1957. That would be four high schools. My school, Dunbar, was to become a junior high school only. They would herd as many African-American students as they could into Horace Mann to avoid having them in any of the other three white high schools. They hoped we would go for the new school rather than integration—going where there were new resources and opportunity.

Their display of white anger got so loud, so public, that Grandma wouldn't allow Conrad to play outside alone for any reason. Both of us were on lockdown.

I intensely followed all the news in the paper and watched the television news. The stories coming out of Little Rock were spreading across the land. I could tell from the reports that the opposition to integration was strong. Each vote they had was negative. Most of the white parents against integration had children in lower grades, so the board of education's plan for integration kept changing.

There were rumors going around about meetings at our churches. White board members were speaking to convince the parents of our community not to send their children to white schools. They threatened that bad things would happen to our entire community if anyone proceeded to push ahead with this.

Papa said, "This is what we call above-board legal threats against our community that if we proceed to exercise our legal civil rights, they are going to punish us."

Grandma said, "This is an invitation to call their bluff. How many times are we going to kowtow? How many chances have we had in the past? How many will we have in the future? We have to go with it now."

While they were home discussing this, I was planning to go to Central High. I had spent so much time imagining what it would be like, how I would get along with the other students there, and the opportunities it would provide. I could imagine that anyone who studied there would get an education fit for a king—or in my case, a queen. I was really looking forward to being in their music department. They had an entire floor dedicated to music, an award-winning band, and a choir. There were lots of instruments. I wanted a music career, and so I wanted to learn about the organ and xylophone and become a fully prepared musician. The school had excellent academic rankings as well. I had heard that they had a huge theater and even put on big musical shows. I kept telling myself that this building was ranked first in the nation in school buildings. I wanted to be there.

In January of 1955, a new governor, Orval Faubus, took over in Arkansas. Some of what he said made me fear that I would never, never get inside Central High School, even though the separate-is-not-equal ruling was law. I held to my thoughts and prayers that no matter who was elected, God was in charge. Grandma said, "Remember, until he proves himself otherwise, assume he is God's child."

But on May 24, 1955, I read that the Little Rock School Board had come up with a new plan to put the lid on integration to Central High School. They weren't going to let African-Americans start attending white schools until September 1957, a full two years away.

Even that faraway integration would be carried out in

three steps. First, our students would be allowed to start at Central High School, which meant grades ten through twelve. If that worked out they would begin integrating grades seven through nine, the junior high students. And if that proved to be okay, they would integrate grades one through six. They would integrate only one school at a time. Around that same time, the Arkansas Board of Education surprised us all by saying that seven state junior colleges would now be open to our undergraduate students.

*Well,* I thought to myself one day as I walked to Dunbar Junior High for my eighth grade class, *at least college classes will be open to us.* I wouldn't have to wait till I could apply for a master's degree, like Mother Lois had. And I even dared to hope that maybe, by the time I got there, college would extend a welcome to me, which no one had done for Mother Lois.

I was surprised that next spring when my teacher, Mrs. Haroldson, asked if anyone in our class lived near Central High School, in that school district. Without thinking, I raised my hand right away. Then she asked which of us wanted to attend Central. I raised my hand once more without a second thought. I was surprised that only a few of my classmates raised their hands.

Mrs. Haroldson passed around a paper asking for phone numbers and addresses of integration volunteers, and I signed my name, not knowing what the future would bring.

Soon after I signed up, I learned that there were more

than a thousand of our students eligible to go. Right off the bat, they said they would screen the applicants heavily in order to choose the right people to go. More than anything, I wanted to be one of their choices—a favored one. My nerves were on edge anytime the phone rang or the mail came. I had to find out first, because I had never told my family I had signed up to start with.

After Rosa Parks's refusal to give up her seat to a white man on an Alabama bus in late 1955, I realized once more the truth of Grandma's words: Sometimes you had to go where you weren't welcome. One woman's actions on a single bus eventually led to the Montgomery, Alabama, bus boycott, a milestone in the Civil Rights Movement. In it, every one of our people in Montgomery, all on the same day, simply refused to ride the bus. The loss of business made the white people who were always so "in charge" realize that our people were gaining strength and that we would not be held down forever.

I felt such a surge of pride when I thought about how my people had banded together to force a change. It gave me hope that maybe things in Little Rock could change. Maybe one day God would give me the strength to help a group of people do something like that.

· · ·

Then one day, the teacher handed me a letter that she said all the volunteers for Central High must take home to their parents. *Oooooops.* I was faced again with the fact that I had held my hand up and volunteered to go to Central High without my parents' permission.

Clutching the letter in my hand, I felt an avalanche of emotions of every possible variety. I thought maybe now I better take volunteering pretty seriously. What if I really got to go? What would happen to me? How would all those almost two thousand white students treat me? I would need new clothes. I knew their music; I didn't know their styles.

But what if the people in the newspaper were right when they said we are stupid? What if their classes were too tough for me? Would they really let me in? Who would go with me?

On the way home, I reread that letter about volunteers attending a meeting at the school board with their parents. I crumpled the paper and tossed it into the trash. Why bother with my dream that had no way of coming true? They would never, never allow us to attend Central High School. That night I

When told that I might attend Central High School, I knew it was a way to get free. I was ready to march forward.

wrote five letters to God, telling Him about my anger and lack of faith. *If you love me,* I wrote, *please, Sir, show me I am equal, equal in every way.*

Despite the fact that I threw the paper away and we didn't attend the meeting, once again my teacher handed me a letter and said, "Okay, Melba, we're counting on you." The letter confirmed that I was among the last sixteen students selected to go to Central High. I just had to find a way to tell my parents and grandmother.

*Yes,* I thought, *this might be my chance to march forward at last.* This was the first step of my dream, and I was determined to take it.

# EPILOGUE

In the end, only nine of us were actually the first to integrate Central High School. My hopes and dreams were all tied in one package as I approached Central High on September 4, 1957. I expected that the adjustment would be similar to attending a new school among my own people. The students

THE LITTLE ROCK NINE

Pictured with me here were my friends, my sisters and brothers, who traveled with me through the historic life-changing event of attending Central High School.

would be different, of course; they wouldn't recognize me. The rules would be different, too, and I would have to work harder to fit in with the academics and with the social scene. Never in a million years could I have imagined that entering Central High School would change absolutely everything in my life. *Integration* was a bigger word than I had thought, a huge word with fire all around it. That first day, my mother and I were met by a mob of hundreds and hundreds of red-faced white people, some of them carrying ropes.

While the adults were threatening to hang one of us, some of the Central High students appeased themselves by hanging an effigy on the front lawn.

There was no space in my head to imagine that we nine would need the same armed forces that had defended us from danger abroad. The Screaming Eagles were young, brave men who gave us outstanding protection.

I got caught up in that mob and experienced a cloud of fear that I had never experienced in my life as Mother and I were chased back to our car by angry, gun-toting men. It would be days and a trip to court later, many news conferences and NAACP meetings, before we could go again. On the second attempt, we were escorted to the side door of the school by Little Rock policemen. Those same policemen had to secretly ferry us out of the basement of the school at the end of the day, past a mob of citizens determined to hang us.

One policeman even suggested that they allow one of us to be given to the mob for hanging as a distraction while the rest escaped, but the man in charge was determined to get us all out. It turned out to be one of the most harrowing events of my life up until that time.

On the third visit to Little Rock's Central High School, we were escorted by the 101st Airborne Division from Fort Campbell, Kentucky, known as the "Screaming Eagles" for their extraordinary military skills. I was really relieved and grateful that President Eisenhower had sent those soldiers to protect us, because how much trouble must we be in, if we needed that much military power? These soldiers came with tons of warring equipment, including helicopters, tanks, jeeps with machine guns, and long rifles with bayonets.

I couldn't sleep; I couldn't eat; I couldn't concentrate. Yet I was required to function at peak every day. I had to crack a smile for the hundreds of reporters taking pictures. Daily I had to function as a student, do my homework, and polish my saddle shoes. Despite the acid thrown in my eyes, the kicking, the tripping, the full-time name calling, and all the other spiteful activities dreamt up by my aggressors, the worst part was the anticipation, the prospect that all these things were going to happen and I didn't know when or where. I do not mean to imply that every one of the 1,900 students there were hostile. Indeed, some were silent, and some tried to befriend us but were immediately punished for their efforts. I was supported daily by the voice of my personal bodyguard, who echoed my grandmother's voice saying, "March forward, girl!"

We were beyond all else trained that there would be no fighting back. We had to take the terrible physical and psychological abuse dealt to us daily with an obedient smile if we were to make it through the year. That experience would see me growing up into an adult with great speed—an adult that had to deeply develop her relationship with God in order to survive.

By Christmastime, we were all operating at the edge. Unfortunately, Minnijean Brown was accused of fighting back and was expelled. Only eight of the nine of us made it through that year.

By the summer of 1958, Governor Faubus, who had been vehemently against integration from the beginning, closed all the high schools in Little Rock for the following school year. During that year, the NAACP worked to get us back

Speaking to reporters became a part of the task of attending Central High School. We were named the number one news story in 1957.

Along with the news reporters, we also had to face outrageously angry protestors who were determined to get rid of us.

into school. Meanwhile, the KKK circulated flyers offering ten thousand dollars dead and five thousand dollars alive for each of us. This was an enormous amount of money, enough to buy a house. So it was decided we had to get out of town.

By luck of the draw, I was sent to Santa Rosa, California, to live with Dr. and Mrs. George McCabe. Suddenly, I found myself with a full white family—a mom and dad, three sisters, and a baby brother—in a totally white community, attending a 99 percent white high school. This school was vastly different from Central High. I made myself a nervous wreck expecting to hear the N word or an attack. No one ever attacked me at Montgomery or said an unkind word.

Instead, they welcomed me with open arms and accepted me as a member of the McCabe family.

The McCabes' acceptance of me and their loving care set my life on a new course of understanding, of dream building, and of knowing that safety is a basic right. Not once did the Klan visit the small farm where we lived. For the first several days at dusk, I would ask why we weren't closing the shades, turning down the lights, and locking the doors. The truth was I was safe and free to dream and work so that I could demonstrate my own personal best. The McCabes would remain my family for the rest of my life.

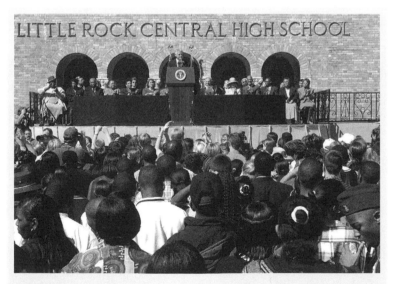

We nine, along with thousands of others, came together to celebrate the fortieth anniversary of the integration of Central High. Because of our experience together, we have always been close and kept in touch through the years.

Looking back over my life, the truth is Grandma was right when she said, "Be patient. God will fulfill your dreams if you are committed and work hard. Just give Him time." As an adult, one of the biggest signs that my eight friends and I had done the right thing in integrating Central High despite the political firestorm it caused in 1957 was visiting the school on the thirtieth anniversary of our entry.

Some of the very townspeople who had oppressed us and kept us from Central High praised and celebrated us. We have since received hundreds of accolades for bravery and commitment to the battle for human rights. I can hardly count the letters I've received saying that my journey through Central High School inspired the letter writers to stand up for their rights.

The Congressional Gold Medal is the highest honor this country awards. It must be voted and approved by members of Congress. By 1997, the United States Congress had voted some 280 Congressional Gold Medals to civilians since its inception in 1776. In November of 1998, it voted to give that prestigious award to me and the eight other black students who integrated Central High School in Little Rock.

In the East Room of the White House on November 8, 1999, I had to pinch myself to see if I was dreaming. I could hardly believe it was me, Melba Pattillo, sitting on a stage in that elegant gold room with its stately place in America's history. President Bill Clinton presided over the cere-

This Congressional Gold Medal was designed specifically for us. We were overwhelmed to join previous recipients such as General George Washington, Charles Lindbergh, Jackie Robinson, Mother Teresa, Pope John Paul II, and Nelson Mandela.

mony, which included crisp-uniformed soldiers from several branches of the military, an endless parade of dignitaries, numerous congressional representatives, members of the press, and family members who had accompanied us there.

I looked around the stage to see the tearful eyes of the other eight. Just like me, Elizabeth Eckford, Terrence Roberts, Ernest Green, Carlotta Walls LaNier, Thelma Mothershed Wair, Gloria Ray Karlmark, Jefferson Thomas, and Minnijean Brown Trickey were now in their midlife. All nine of us had been friends prior to our adventure together, and had known one another since elementary school. We were chosen to integrate Central High all those years ago on the basis of grades, past performance, and behavior. We have grown up to become teachers, psychologists, accountants, news reporters, and published authors. Today, we are parents and some of us are grandparents. We are all equally surprised that we have been designated civil rights icons who changed history in the eyes of historians and the American people.

We smiled at one another that day in the White House as the speakers on the program lavished us with praise for our courage in surviving that school year in Central High School. My name was called. Cameras flashed. I rose and approached

This day is forever etched in our minds. The fact that we received this incredible honor confirmed that indeed we had taken the right action by moving forward through this dangerous task.

the president of the United States of America. He embraced me and handed me the heavy gold object—a work of art created by the United States Mint—that bore my name and the image of the nine of us climbing the front steps of Central High. I was humbled at the sight of it. This medal, this ceremony—this incredible moment—was one more affirmation that indeed, as my Grandmother India told me, there are times when YOU MUST GO WHERE YOU'RE NOT WELCOME, or you will become trapped in the places where others assign you.

Through it all, through the applause and the lights and the pomp and circumstance, I remembered that I was just a little girl from Little Rock, Arkansas—a girl my grandma called a baby warrior—who once was forced to ride in the back of city buses and drink only from a water fountain marked COLORED.

Most of all, my grandmother taught me, indeed as the Disney song says, "A dream is a wish your heart makes when you're fast asleep." Each and every one of us has a right to dream and to strive to make our dreams come true.

# NOTE TO READERS

After reading this book, some of you may conclude that I hold a grudge against white people in general. At age sixteen, when I felt crushed by the students at Central High School, thinking that those outside would see me fail, and after a year of being home alone, I was taken in by a white family. George and Kay McCabe put their hearts and souls into parenting me and launching me into adulthood. No one could have given me more strength and love than this family. To this day, I am proud to say I remain a member of the McCabe family.

When I meet new people, no matter their race or religion, I assume we meet each other in love. I know that love is the only answer to guiding any relationship.

To this day, I love my second mother and father with all my heart. Their children are still my close brother and sisters. It was in the McCabes' loving arms that I learned that we are all equal when we decide to be so.

# ACKNOWLEDGMENTS

I am most grateful for the attention, compassion, and love of the people below, who have eased my pathway along my journey:

My children, Kellie Beals and Matthew and Evan Pattillo, who were my teachers and who taught me so many spiritual lessons and continue to fill my life with challenge and joy.

Grandmother India Peyton, whose wisdom and love of God sustain me each day.

Mother, Dr. Lois Pattillo, whose strength and belief in education and endless possibilities fuel my struggles to achieve and serve.

Carol and George McCabe, who were willing to introduce me to proclaiming and sustaining my own equality despite objections and hardships posed by society.

My McCabe sisters and brothers, Judy, Joan, Dori, and Rick, and especially Judy's children, Sara, Mark, Todd, and Trey, and grandchildren, Cody, Zack, and Kellie, who all shower me with love and acceptance.

My brother, Conrad Pattillo, a black man in a blue uniform, who has contributed to social advances through his career as the first African-American Arkansas state police officer to receive a presidential appointment as the United States Marshal for the Eastern District of Arkansas

Judie Fouchaux, my executive assistant, whose compassion and deep understanding of humanity sustained me through my reflections on my harrowing and gut-wrenching past.

Pauline and Richard France, whose prayers and consistent visits have supported me through this journey.

Carol Normandy, who dried my tears and convinced me that I could survive and benefit from recalling sad memories of my youth.

Shane and Michael McLennan for their loving kindness and for Shane's many visits and gifts of joy and peace, and as testimony to how one defines a good neighbor no matter the racial divide.

Attorney Sanford J. Rosen, who has dedicated his life to attaining civil rights for those who need him most.